PALACES OF
ST. PETERSBURG
RUSSIAN IMPERIAL STYLE

PALACES
of
ST. PETERSBURG

Russian Imperial Style

Presented by

THE MISSISSIPPI COMMISSION FOR INTERNATIONAL CULTURAL EXCHANGE, INC.

In Association With
THE STATE MUSEUM RESERVE PETERHOF
THE STATE MUSEUM TSARSKOJE SELO
THE MUSEUM PRESERVE GATCHINA PALACE
THE STATE MUSEUM RESERVE PAVLOVSK PALACE AND PARK

MISSISSIPPI ARTS PAVILION
March 1—August 31, 1996
Jackson, Mississippi

PAGES 2-3:
The Grand Palace at Peterhof, the "Summer Capital" of the Russian Empire, is justly celebrated for its magnificent cascading fountains.

PAGES 4-5:
The impressive facade and formal gardens of the Catherine Palace at Tsarskoje Selo ("Tsar's Village") are the work of several successive generations of master architects, craftsmen, and designers imported from Italy, France, England, and throughout the Russian Empire.

PAGES 6-7:
The masculine facade of Gatchina Palace, originally built for Catherine the Great's lover, Count Grigori Orlov, is tempered by the natural beauty of its English-style parkland setting.

PAGES 8-9:
Originally planned as a country residence for Catherine the Great's son and heir, Grand Duke Paul (Pavel) Petrovich, Pavlovsk is considered a gem of Russian classicism, combining elements of Italian Palladian style with the vernacular of traditional Russian country-estate design.

PAGE 10:
The stunning "Imperial Gatchina Palace Egg," encrusted with seed pearls and containing a miniature replica of Gatchina Palace, was created circa 1902 by Fabergé master Mikhail Evlampievich Perchin. It is on loan to the exhibition courtesy of the Walters Art Gallery of Baltimore.

FRONT COVER:
Seen from the Grand Canal, the baroque majesty of the Grand Palace and Grand Cascade at Peterhof bears vivid testament to Peter the Great's desire to build an imperial complex to rival that of Versailles. Photo/Winnie Denker.

BACK COVER:
Designed by Bartolomeo Rastrelli for Empress Elizabeth Petrovna, this elaborate wood-carved and gilded door surround from the Portrait Hall of the Catherine Palace incorporates symbols of imperial Russia, including the Romanov double-headed eagle and the imperial crown. Photo/Leonid Bogdanov.

PHOTOGRAPHY
All photographs by
Carlos Domenech

(except photos on pages 42, 127, 136, 142, 143, 145, and 146 by Leonid Bogdanov; pages 4, 5, and 70 by Winnie Denker).

Copyright © 1996 The Mississippi Commission for International Cultural Exchange, Inc.

Produced by Thomasson-Grant, Inc., Charlottesville, Virginia

Printed in Hong Kong.

Library of Congress Cataloging-in-Publication Data available.

ISBN 1-56566-105-2
Hardcover

ISBN 1-56566-106-0
Softcover

Sponsors

SKYTEL

DEPOSIT GUARANTY NATIONAL BANK

This project has been partially funded through the generous assistance of the State of Mississippi through the Mississippi Department of Economic & Community Development, Division of Tourism; Metro Jackson Convention & Visitors Bureau; and the City of Jackson.

Palaces of St. Petersburg

Sponsors

Major Sponsors

Delta Air Lines, Inc.
Jackson Coca-Cola Bottling Company
Jitney Jungle Stores of America, Inc.
Trustmark National Bank

Sponsors

BellSouth
Chevron Companies
Entergy
Sam's Town Hotel & Gambling Hall
The Clarion-Ledger

Patrons

Blue Cross/Blue Shield of MS
Irby Companies

Contributors

Bank of Mississippi
Thomas W. Bobbitt and Associates, P.A., Landscape Architects
Bryan Foods
The Edison Walthall Hotel
Hancock Fabrics
Harvey Hotel, Downtown Jackson
Junior League of Jackson, Inc.
MMI Hotel Group
Mississippi Consortium for International Development
Newsprint South, Inc.
St. Dominic Health Services, Inc.
Siemens Medical Systems
The Walker Foundation

AAA Printers•AIA Mississippi•Ameristar Casino•Nanette Watkins-Andrews•BWI of Jackson•Barefield & Company•Beechill Nursery, Yazoo City•Zoia Belyakova•Donna Biggert•George Benashvili, M.D.•Beverly A. Bolton•Bravo! Restaurant•Brennan's Restaurant•Brown's Fine Art & Framing, Inc.•Capital Concrete Cutting, Inc. (Terry and Rita Beckham)•Century Cellunet•Cochran-Sysco•Commander's Palace Restaurant•Cowboy Maloney's Electric City•Creative Marketing•Mr. and Mrs. Emanuel Crystal•Delta Queen Steamboat Company•Deposit Guaranty Marketing Dept.•Discount Nursery and Landscaping•Edwin Dodd, M.D.•Dunn Construction Company, Inc., Mike Harrell and Tom Black•Dutch Brothers Greenhouses, Lucedale•Elisnore Garden Club•Emporium Cafe•Frito-Lay, Inc.•Galloway Memorial United Methodist Church•Garry Graves Landscapes•Georgia-Pacific Corporation•Gil Ford Photography•Grand Casinos•Graphic Reproduction•Greenbrook Florist•Green Oak Nursery, Inc.•Gulf Coast Council of Garden Clubs•HADCO-Bob and Lois Landry•Harper, Rains, Stokes & Knight, CPAs•Dr. and Mrs. R. Brent Harrison•Herrin-Gear•Hinds Community College Landscape Management Technology Program•Mr. and Mrs. Warren A. Hood•Jackson Lighting Center, Gary and Verba Clark•Jackson Paper Company•Jefcoat Fence Company, Kurt Rushing•Walter T. Johnson•Keep Jackson Beautiful, Barbara Ryan•Kinko's Copies of Jackson•David J. Koenig•Life & Safety Service•Senator Trent Lott•MCTA•Madison Central High School Air Force Junior ROTC•Magnolia Federal Bank for Savings•Edward R. Malayan, Embassy of the Russian Federation•Mr. and Mrs. William D. Mann•McClure Lawn Irrigation, Inc., Phil Wilson•Mr. John McGowan•Med South•Methodist Medical Center•MicroData Corporation•Millsaps Buie House•Mississippi Air National Guard•Mississippi Bottle Water•Mississippi College Band, Dr. John Hanberry, Director•Mississippi Cooperative Extension Service Research and Extension, Raymond•Mississippi Materials Company•Mississippi Nurserymen's Association•Mississippi Secretary of State's Office•Mississippi Symphony Orchestra, Colman Pearce, Conductor•Mississippi Tourism Promotion Association•MISSLOU Brick Manufacturers Association•MobileComm•Robert Mondavi•Congressman G. V. "Sonny" Montgomery•Natchez Convention & Visitors Bureau•Natchez Eola Hotel•Nebletts Frame Shop•Nick Strickland's Quick Print•Billy Neville, The Rogue•New Orleans Museum of Art•Phillips Bark Processing, Bill Phillips•Honorable Thomas J. Pickering, Ambassador of the United States of America•Roger Prigent, Malmaison Antiques•Ramada Inn Metro•Raymond High School Air Force Junior ROTC•Rocky Creek Nursery, Inc., Lucedale•E. J. Russell, Secretary of the Senate•Margaret Sandifer, Department of Agriculture•Scalamandre•Sedgwick James of Mississippi, Inc.•Sherwood Forest Garden Club•Southern Electric Corporation, Steve Weaver•Steel Services Corporation•Mr. Ernest M. Steen•The Office Supply Company•Tupelo Daily Journal•United States Army Herald Trumpets, Lt. Col. Tony Cason, Director•U. S. Axminster•Vickers, Inc.•Vicksburg Convention & Visitors Bureau•Walgreen Companies•Patti Ware•Windsor Court Hotel.

Contents

PETERHOF *24*

CATHERINE PALACE *72*

GATCHINA *126*

PAVLOVSK *152*

Foreword

By Jack L. Kyle

Executive Director, Palaces of St. Petersburg: Russian Imperial Style

The saga of the development of the exhibition *Palaces of St. Petersburg: Russian Imperial Style* is as uplifting and inspiring as the development of the four participating palace-museums themselves: Peterhof, Catherine Palace at Tsarskoje Selo, Gatchina, and Pavlovsk. In both cases, it is the story of mankind's ability to create and achieve.

The *Palaces of St. Petersburg: Russian Imperial Style* exhibition is the direct result of a humanitarian effort between the State of Mississippi and the City of St. Petersburg, Russia, via their respective medical communities, led by St. Petersburg neurosurgeon Dr. Yuri N. Zubkov, on the one hand, and William M. Stevens, chairman of Mississippians Reaching Out and the Mississippi Commission for International Cultural Exchange, Inc., on the other.

Through this humanitarian activity, the idea for an international cultural exchange was born and promulgated by a delegation of Mississippians who visited St. Petersburg in the summer of 1993. Among those early participants was Mississippi's First Lady, Mrs. Pat Fordice, who has contributed her support and inspiration to the development of this project. The exhibition has also received much support from the mayor of St. Petersburg, Anatoly A. Sobchak, and his wife, Ludmila.

Considered to be the largest cultural project ever undertaken by the State of Mississippi, this tremendous endeavor would never have come to fruition without the support of the Mississippi Legislature, Governor and Mrs. Kirk Fordice, the City of Jackson and its mayor, Kane Ditto, and the keen involvement of the Mississippi business community, particularly in the persons of John N. Palmer, chief executive officer of MTEL/Skytel, and E. B. Robinson, Jr., chairman and chief executive officer of Deposit Guaranty National Bank.

Inspired by the grandeur and historical importance of the four great palaces that have graciously participated in this project, *Palaces of St. Petersburg: Russian Imperial Style* would never have been realized without the further inspiration of being able to share this rich cultural legacy with hundreds of thousands of school students and other visitors from around the world.

In order to best convey to the visitor to the exhibition the unique architectural and decorative character of these four great imperial palaces, the skills of numerous Russian artisans—along with those of many Americans—were enlisted in full measure. Master woodcarvers and sculptors, among others, were engaged to re-create elaborate parquet floors, baroque wood-carved decorations, and replicas of sculptures, mantels, and objets d'art. The stunning results will give the visitor to the exhibition an inside glimpse of the magnificence of these great palaces—which are, in reality, not only Russian historical monuments, but *world* monuments.

The largest Russian exhibition ever presented (showcasing over six hundred objects!), *Palaces of St. Petersburg: Russian Imperial Style* is the result of the joint effort of the respective directors of Peterhof (Dr. Vadim V. Znamenov), Catherine Palace at Tsarskoje Selo (Mr. Ivan P. Sautov), Gatchina (Dr. Nikolai S. Tretyakov), and Pavlovsk (Dr. Yuri V. Mudrov), as well as their talented staffs, all of whom have contributed countless hours to bring about this exhibition.

From a curatorial aspect, I would like to express particular appreciation to Ms. Nina Vernova, deputy director and chief curator at Peterhof; Dr. Victor M. Faybisovitch, deputy director, and Ms. Larisa V. Bardovskaya, chief curator, at the Catherine Palace at Tsarskoje Selo; Ms. Galina N. Kondakova, deputy director of Gatchina Palace; and Ms. Ludmila V. Koval, deputy director at Pavlovsk Palace.

A special note of appreciation must be extended to Dr. Gary E. Vikan, director of the Walters Art Gallery, Baltimore, Maryland, and his board of trustees for loaning the Fabergé "Imperial Gatchina Palace Egg."

May I call special attention to the resolve of the executive committee of the Mississippi Commission for International Cultural Exchange, Inc., namely, William L. Stevens, chairman, William D. Mounger, honorary chairman, Thomas B. Shepherd, III, Douglas C. Rule, and Thomas Pittman for their wise counsel and guidance. I would also like to express my gratitude to William M. Jones for his dedication to the project and to Susan S. Harrison for her efforts.

No endeavor of this magnitude could ever have succeeded without the dedication of a talented and capable staff, with which I have been greatly blessed, along with the assistance of a magnificent team of volunteers, without whom this project could not have been presented.

There are countless other individuals and entities who have offered goodwill, support, and assistance whose names lack of space precludes me from mentioning. To you and all who have played a role in the *Palaces of St. Petersburg: Russian Imperial Style* exhibition, please savor the thought that you have contributed in some part to the betterment of mankind.

A Letter From the Director

I am thrilled to welcome the American public to this unique exhibition. Without leaving the USA, visitors will be able to see firsthand some of the most celebrated examples of our culture—examples embodied in the famous palace and park ensembles of imperial Russia.

Among them, perhaps the best-known is the imperial residence of Peterhof, located in the "suburbs" of St. Petersburg. Founded by Peter the Great in the early eighteenth century as a "Russian Versailles," for two centuries the palace complex served as the summer capital of all Russia.

Peterhof's palaces, parks, and, of course, the world-renowned fountain and cascade system, attract up to six million guests annually from all quarters of the globe. They come not only to enjoy the beauty of art, but the magnificence of nature, as well. More importantly, the fate of the former imperial residence is a mirror reflection of the history and culture of Russia itself.

Planned and executed as a monument to the glory of Mother Russia, Peterhof was occupied in 1941-1944 by Nazi troops, who plundered and destroyed what had taken centuries to create. The rebirth of this architectural gem has become a symbol of the immortality of our culture.

Lately, we are glad to welcome an ever-widening stream of foreign tourists and official guests, including a growing number of Americans—a testament to the positive relations between our peoples today. I am sure that this cultural exchange will continue to be mutually pleasant—and enlightening—for all.

—*Dr. Vadim V. Znamenov*

CATHERINE PALACE
(TSARSKOJE SELO)
A Letter From the Director

Each of the unique imperial residences in the environs of St. Petersburg has left behind a singular blueprint of the changing artistic tastes and styles of almost three centuries of Russian art and architecture. The genius of the master architects, craftsmen, and artisans enlisted by the Russian tsars and tsarinas is embodied in these celebrated imperial ensembles. The beautiful parkland and gardens surrounding these splendid palaces not only serve to frame and complement the structures themselves, but also to embody the philosophical ideals of our predecessors concerning the harmony between man and nature.

The imperial palaces, which by the beginning of the twentieth century had come to house priceless treasures from every corner of the globe, suffered dramatic losses following the revolution of 1917 and, especially, during the years of the Second World War. Miraculously, a legion of Russian restorers and workmen have re-created much from the ruins. But it is not worth talking about the renewed splendor of these St. Petersburg residences; they must be seen!

At the exhibition, two interiors of the Catherine Palace have been lovingly re-created: the Portrait Hall, a masterpiece of the Russian baroque style, and the Blue Formal Drawing Room, a brilliant study in the neo-classical idiom. Although these are only two rooms of hundreds at Tsarskoje Selo, we consider the "Palaces of St. Petersburg" exhibition to be a perfect first step in getting acquainted with the palace and park ensembles of the Russian imperial family. We hope that after visiting the exhibition in Jackson, Mississippi, you will be motivated to visit Russia. We shall be glad to see you at Tsarskoje Selo.

—*Dr. Ivan P. Sautov*

A Letter From the Director

ever before has the American public been given the opportunity to see so many historic relics of Russia in its own country! Some of the most culturally significant artifacts of our most celebrated imperial estates—Peterhof, Tsarskoje Selo, Gatchina, and Pavlovsk—have traveled half way around the world to grace this exhibition in Jackson, Mississippi.

Although the proprietors of these wonderful architectural monuments have changed over the years, each succeeding generation of Russian citizens has learned to appreciate anew the treasures of its imperial past through these great palaces—and now the American public can, too.

One of our country's most unusual—and romantic—palaces, Gatchina is, sadly, still in the slow process of its rebirth. The Second World War destroyed its priceless interiors, and, unfortunately, reconstruction has only just begun.

Nevertheless, we are glad to represent the Gatchina Palace at the exhibition with a re-creation of the Throne Hall, a monumental example of the best of our imperial past, as well as by a gallery of beautiful objets d'art—tapestries, paintings, antique armaments, and porcelains.

I am sure that this exhibition of some of Russia's most important palaces will entice visitors from the USA to visit Gatchina for years to come. We are looking forward to it.

—Dr. Nikolai S. Tretyakov

A Letter From the Director

 e are extremely pleased with the great interest the American public has shown in our Russian culture. For the first time, without leaving the United States, Americans can get acquainted with the treasures of Pavlovsk Palace, which was the first of the imperial Russian residences to be restored after World War II. Its harmonious tranquility, the purity of its neo-classical style, the first-class collections that fill its halls, and the shady alleys of the magnificent park which surrounds it have conquered the hearts of visitors from around the world. Among the many Americans who have visited have been Presidents Nixon, Carter, and Reagan, as well as the brilliant pianist Van Cliburn, who played the antique piano which had once belonged to the Empress Maria Fyodorovna.

The popularity of the palace has grown enormously with the American public over the years, particularly after Suzanne Massie published *Pavlovsk: The Life of a Russian Palace* (1990). It was the first time a foreign writer had told the incredible story of one of our country's most celebrated royal retreats, a history not only of the residents themselves, but also of the legions of talented artisans who have given it a second lease on life.

In the exhibition you will see the re-creation of one of the most poetic interiors of Pavlovsk: the Lantern Study, one of the favorite rooms of Maria Fyodorovna. And in the Pavlovsk "Gallery" you will see a number of masterpieces especially created or purchased for this imperial estate. We hope you will be inspired to see more on our shores.

—Dr. Yuri V. Mudrov

PALACES OF
ST. PETERSBURG

RUSSIAN IMPERIAL STYLE

Peterhof

In 1703, under the thunder of cannons along the Baltic coast of Europe, a new capital of Russia emerged—St. Petersburg. Built by Peter I ("the Great") as a "window on the West," the city's prominence would always be conditioned by its proximity to water. It is not surprising, then, that Russia's tsars chose to situate their imperial residences by the sea, the access to which Peter I had felt assured would usher in a whole new epoch in Russian culture. He was not wrong.

Peterhof was founded as early as 1705, when Peter I decided to establish his official summer residence along the shores of the Gulf of Finland. By 1715, the construction of two palaces—Monplaisir and the future "Grand" Palace—had been started. Two areas of parkland—the Lower Park and the Upper Gardens—had been laid out along terraces that sloped to the sea. A short time later, two smaller palaces—the Hermitage and Marli—were also erected. But it was the ensemble of fountains and cascades that became the real gem of Peterhof. Brilliantly designed and executed, the fountain system for Peter the Great's residence, which had already been nicknamed the "Russian Versailles," placed the whole complex among the world's finest masterpieces of palace and park design.

The cupola of this gem-like pavilion at Peterhof is adorned with a gilded weather vane in the form of a double-headed Romanov eagle.

Beginning with the solemn ceremony in 1723 that marked Peterhof's completion, the imperial residence would be considered the summer capital of the Russian Empire for the next two hundred years. During this time, palaces and pavilions were constructed one after another for each succeeding tsar or tsarina, until the last palace for the last tsar, Nicholas II, was assembled at the end of the nineteenth century.

Outside, parks were studded with a multitude of marble and bronze sculptures created by a long list of outstanding Russian and European masters. Inside, richly decorated interiors housed a vast collection of paintings and decorative objects that had been ambitiously gathered by a royal family which had a distinct taste for luxury.

In 1917, after the February revolution overthrew the tsar, the Provisional Government decided to turn the palaces and parks of Peterhof into a huge working museum, enabling the larger Russian public to see the splendor of imperial culture for the first time. The complicated work of devising inventories, descriptions, and the study of the colossal number of artifacts of the former residence had begun in earnest. Nevertheless, this work came to an abrupt halt by October, when the Bolsheviks came

to power. Within a year, however, the new government again turned Peterhof into a museum. Millions more people were given the possibility to visit the former Romanov palaces for a token entrance fee. The treasures of Peterhof seemed inexhaustible, but by the beginning of the 1930s, the Bolsheviks were confiscating and selling abroad a considerable amount of the palace's outstanding art objects.

Disaster really struck on September 23, 1941, when Peterhof was occupied for the first time by German Nazi troops. For nine hundred days, the Nazis plundered and destroyed everything that the museum staff had not managed to evacuate. When, in January 1944, Russian soldiers entered the destroyed palace complex, it seemed that this gem of imperial Russia had gasped its last breath.

With a steely determination that had marked the entire country's resistance to the Germans during the war, restoration began soon after 1945—and is still going on today! The collections that had been safely evacuated again took their rightful places in the restored rooms of the palaces, and sculptures were again placed on the steps of the cascades and in the alleys of the parks. The lost objects were replaced by similar ones from the palaces and museums of St. Petersburg proper, and hundreds of objects which had disappeared from Peterhof in the 1930s were found and returned.

At present, the Museum Reserve Peterhof comprises three parks and six palace-museums, as well as the art gallery. Tens of thousands of potential exhibition items are still being kept in storage, waiting for the completion of the restorations of several more residences. Today, the museums of Peterhof are among the most highly visited in Europe, with six million visitors a year, and as many as a hundred thousand people in a single day.

The museum has sent dozens of exhibitions all over the world, and, although this is not the first time an exhibition has traveled to America, the marvelous show in Jackson, Mississippi, is the first time so much has been on display in one venue at one time. We at Peterhof hope it will be the first of many encore performances.

—*Dr. Vadim V. Znamenov,*
Director, Peterhof

Yellow Banqueting Hall

The Yellow Banqueting Hall, meticulously re-created for the present exhibition, is one of the most significant interiors of the Peterhof complex known as the Catherine Block. Although this separate palace is not the largest structure at Peterhof, it is nevertheless one of the most important in all Russia.

The Catherine Block is part of an isolated complex of buildings united under the common name "Ensemble of Monplaisir," originally the name of the first small structure Peter I built in what is known as the "Lower Park." In the beginning, the site was a mere vegetable garden, and later a small stone orangerie was constructed in its place. In 1748, on the foundation of this orangerie, the architect Bartolomeo Rastrelli, the darling of the imperial family, created a new palace for the empress Elizabeth Petrovna that would be large enough for the elaborate receptions and balls of which the tsarina was so fond. The main facade of the new palace faced the "Monplaisir Garden" and featured a formal porch, the doors of which led to the Lower Park. The interiors were done up in the grandest baroque style.

The original decoration of these interiors gave way by 1785 to the lighter, neo-classical designs of the Italian architect Giacomo Quarenghi, who had been invited to work in Russia by Catherine, the wife of Tsar Peter III. On June 28, 1762, Catherine, then known as the Grand Duchess, had left this house at Peterhof, returning a day later escorted by her guardsmen to overthrow her husband. This small but bloody coup made the former German princess, now known as Catherine "the Great," empress of all Russia. To commemorate the event, the palace was renamed the "Catherine Block," and soon was being used for the formal receptions, dinners, and annual balls that marked the graduation ceremonies for the alumnae of the Smolny Institute of the Noble Ladies, which had been established by Catherine soon after she came to power.

The main room of this historically significant palace is the huge Yellow Banqueting Hall, exquisitely decorated in the neo-classical style by Quarenghi. Its walls are punctuated by sixteen pairs of Corinthian pilasters, with molded ornaments featuring a classical vase and a female figure in an oval medallion decorating the space between each pair. Over the four doors in the room are bas-relief sculptures by the master Jacques-Dominique Rachette that allegorically glorify architecture and science, music and theater.

But it is not only this spendid architectural detail for which the Yellow Banqueting Hall is justly celebrated. More important is the display of Russian imperial porcelain, laid out on the table in the center of the room. Fired and decorated at the St. Petersburg Imperial Porcelain Works, founded as early as the middle of the eighteenth century, it includes more than 4,500 pieces of some of the finest china ever created. Known as the "Gouriev Service," after Count Gouriev, who commissioned the service in 1809-1817 for the court of Alexander I, the gloriously preserved pieces can be considered an illustrated encyclopedia of Russian history. The plates are painted with dozens of images of the various peoples of Russia, and other pieces—such as the wine

coolers—feature views of St. Petersburg, its environs, and Moscow.

Complementing this magnificent display of imperial luxury, walls of the Banqueting Hall are decorated with portraits of Catherine II and Alexander I by the English painter George Dawe. The portrait of Peter I is part of a huge tapestry, woven in Paris in the beginning of the nineteenth century after a painting by Charles Steuben, that depicts the legendary rescue of fishermen by Peter the Great during a storm on the Ladoga Sea outside St. Petersburg. The tapestry had been commissioned by Napoleon, but was completed under the reign of Louis XVIII, who presented it to Alexander I.

Another event of Russian history is commemorated in the design of a clock, which replicates the famous sculptural monument to Minin and Pozharsky on Red Square in Moscow. The clock was created by the celebrated French bronzemaster Pierre-Philippe Thomir and is considered the best of the collection of artistic bronzeware housed in the Catherine Block.

Today, the Catherine Block is renowned not only for its history and architectural decoration, but also for its collections of applied decorative arts: Russian furniture (created from the designs of well-known architects such as Carlo Rossi and Andrei Voronikhin), the Russian porcelain and French bronzeware, and the thousands of other precious objects created for or bought by Catherine the Great.

—*Nina N. Vernova,*
Deputy Director, Peterhof

Palaces of St. Petersburg

Palaces of St. Petersburg

LEFT: GEORGE DAWE. PORTRAIT OF TSAR ALEXANDER I. 1825.
OIL ON CANVAS. 240.5 X 152.2. INV. NO. PDMP 758-ZH.
Rewarded in 1828 with the title "Chief Portrait Painter of His Imperial Highness" for executing this commanding likeness of Alexander I in the uniform of the Cavalry Guards Regiment, Dawe had been commissioned to paint over four hundred portraits of Russia's military brass following the Napoleonic Wars.

ABOVE: VIGILIUS ERICHSEN. CATHERINE II ASTRIDE "BRILLIANT." 1778.
OIL ON CANVAS. INV. NO. GRM-5378.
A smaller copy of a canvas which hangs in the Throne Hall of the Grand Palace, this painting depicts Catherine the Great's historic return to Peterhof following the palace coup in 1762 which made her empress.

TAPESTRY "PETER THE GREAT DURING THE STORM ON THE LADOGA SEA."
ROYAL TAPESTRY MANUFACTORY. PARIS. 1810s.
WOOL, SILK, HANDWEAVING. 390 X 350. INV. NO. 277-TK.
Woven after a celebrated painting by Charles Steuben depicting Peter I courageously commanding a vessel during the war against Sweden, this tapestry was commissioned by Napoleon as a gift to Alexander I. It is among the most valuable objects of the Peterhof collection and hangs today in the Monplaisir Palace.

THREE-CANDLE SCONCE (ONE OF A PAIR). RUSSIA. 1770-1810.
CHASED GILDED BRONZE, PAINTED IRON. 48.9 X 40 X 3. INV. NO. PDMP 1252-MT.

CLOCK "MININ AND POZHARSKY." PIERRE-PHILIPPE THOMIRE. PARIS. 1815-1820.
MARBLE, BRONZE, GILDING. 104 X 77 X 27. INV. NO. PDMP 874-MT.
One of the best of the many reproductions of I. P. Martos's famous monument "Minin and Pozharsky" in Red Square, this important bronze masterwork was commissioned in a burst of patriotic enthusiasm following Russia's defeat of Napoleon in 1812.

CANDELABRUM WITH A FIGURE OF NIKE BLOWING A HORN (ONE OF A PAIR). PIERRE-VICTOR LEDURE. PARIS. 1745-1810.
GILDED AND PATINATED BRONZE. HEIGHT-105. BASE-18.3 X 18.5. TOP-30 X 30. INV. NO. PDMP 2027-MT.

TABLE KNIVES AND FORKS. G. A. BERNSTROM, M. KARPINSKY. (GOURIEV SERVICE.) ST. PETERSBURG. 1827-1829.
GILDED SILVER, CARVED JASPER. INV. NOS. PDMP 84-DM, 87-98-DM.
Part of the "Gouriev Service," which often traveled with the imperial family, some of the handles were replaced after being broken during a trip in 1848.

RIGHT: DINNER PLATES. UNMARKED (GOURIEV SERVICE). IMPERIAL PORCELAIN WORKS. ST. PETERSBURG. 1809-1817.
PORCELAIN, OVERGLAZE MONOCHROME GROUND, GOLD PAINTING, TOOLING, AND OVERGLAZE POLYCHROME DECORATION IN THE CAVETTOS. DIAMETER-25.
Featuring scenes and peoples from everyday life—"Resting Cossacks" (opposite), "Sayan Tartars," "Easter Egg Peddlers," "Vagrant Sawyer and Pie Peddler," "A Merchant's Wife From Kaluga," etc.—this set of twenty-eight dinner plates was a virtual ethnographic encyclopedia of Russia and was usually reserved for foreign diplomatic receptions.

DINNER PLATES. UNMARKED (GOURIEV SERVICE). IMPERIAL PORCELAIN WORKS. ST. PETERSBURG. 1809-1817.
PORCELAIN, OVERGLAZE MONOCHROME GROUND, GOLD PAINTING, TOOLING. DIAMETER-25.

Part of the magnificent "Gouriev Service" purchased for the most formal of occasions during the reign of Alexander I, these plates are three examples of a complete set of twenty-four. The entire service includes over 4,500 pieces.

These and
preceding pages:
Commissioned in 1809-
1817 and named after the
Minister of the Imperial
Cabinet, the "Gouriev
Service" was created by
the best artisans at the
Imperial Porcelain Works
in St. Petersburg. With
most of the items pro-
duced in sets of twenty-
four, the complete set was
enlarged during the reign
of Nicholas II (1894-
1917) to include more
coffee, tea, and dessert
services, including some
of the exquisite fruit com-
potes featured on this
page.

Palaces of St. Petersburg

LEFT:
ICE BUCKET (ONE OF FOUR). UNMARKED (GOURIEV SERVICE). IMPERIAL PORCELAIN WORKS. ST. PETERSBURG. 1809-1817.
PORCELAIN, OVERGLAZE MONOCHROME GROUND, GOLD PAINTING, TOOLING, OVERGLAZE POLYCHROME PAINTING. HEIGHT-39. INV. NO. PDMP 3321-F.

ABOVE: NIKOLAI IVANOVICH SVERCHKOV. PORTRAIT OF TSAR ALEXANDER II. 1876.
OIL ON CANVAS. 71 X 95. INV. NO. PDMP 1124-ZH.

RIGHT: PETER PETROVICH ZABOLOTSKY. <u>PORTRAIT OF TSAR ALEXANDER III</u>. 1889.
OIL ON CANVAS. 172 X 110. INV. NO. GRM-ZB 1938.
The painter was awarded with the Imperial Academy of Fine Arts's prestigious Gold Medal after completing this portrait, which features the popular tsar in the full military regalia of the Cavalry Guards Regiment.

LEFT: G. BOTTMAN. <u>PORTRAIT OF TSAR NICHOLAS I</u>. 1849.
OIL ON CANVAS. 103 X 75. INV. NO. PDMP 929-ZH.
Rewarded with the title of "Academician" in 1853 after executing this military-style portrait, Bottman subsequently painted another for the Gatchina Palace. Both feature Nicholas I's favorite dog, aptly named "Hussar," lying at his feet.

RIGHT: ERNST-FRIEDRICH KARLOVICH VON LIPGART. <u>PORTRAIT OF TSAR NICHOLAS II</u>. C. 1900.
OIL ON CANVAS. 103 X 80.5. INV. NO GRM-ZB 1910.
An arts scholar and the chief curator of the Winter Palace after 1905, von Lipgart executed a number of portraits and decorative compositions for the palace, including this classic portrait of Russia's last tsar.

ABOVE: PETER PETROVICH ZABOLOTSKY. <u>PORTRAIT OF THE EMPRESS MARIA FYODOROVNA</u>. 1883.
OIL ON CANVAS. 169 X 167. INV. NO GRM-ZB 1939.
A perfect foil to the militaristic theme of the painter's portrait of her husband, Alexander III, the Danish-born tsarina is the quintessence of femininity in white satin and lace.

**TWO CUPS.
STOCKHOLM. 1690-
1700**

SILVER, GILDING, FILI-
GREE, GARNETS. HEIGHT-
18.5. INV. NOS. PDMP
18-DM, 19-DM.

Two of the most precious
of Peter the Great's per-
sonal belongings, these
exquisitely wrought silver
and garnet-studded cups
were moved from the
Winter Palace to Peterhof
by order of Tsar
Nicholas I in 1829.

**ABOVE AND RIGHT:
DRESSING MIRROR
AND CANDELABRUM
(ONE OF TWO).
MIRROR—FRANÇOIS-
THOMAS GERMAIN.
PARIS. 1748-1755.
CANDELABRUM—J. F.
KEPPING.
ST. PETERSBURG.
1750-1751.**

BOTH—SILVER, CHASING,
CARVING. HEIGHT (MIR-
ROR)-81.5; (CANDE-
LABRUM)-34.5.
INVENTORY NOS. PDMP
81-DM; 188-DM.

Featuring the coat-of-
arms of the Russian
imperial family, two elab-
orately wrought candle-
sticks were commissioned
to complement the silver
mirror, which, according
to legend, had been a gift
from Louis XV of France
to Empress Elizabeth
Petrovna.

**INKSET. M. A.
CHIZHOV. PETERHOF
LAPIDARY WORKS.
1875.**

SILVER, CHASING, CARV-
ING, JASPER, ROMAN
MOSAIC. HEIGHT-56. INV.
NOS. PDMP 48/1,2-DM,
1026/1,2-DM.

To mark the re-opening
of the Peterhof Lapidary
Works on July 26, 1875,
this inkset, in the form of
a monument to
Catherine the Great, was
presented to Alexander
II, who used it in his
study at Peterhof.

Palaces of St. Petersburg

LEFT: BOAT SUN-CLOCK. JOHN ROWLEY. LONDON. 1715.
SILVER, COPPER, CHASING, ENGRAVING, GLASS. HEIGHT-45. INV. NO. PDMP 505-DM. Prepared by order of King George I of England as a diplomatic gift for Peter I, this intricately designed compass-cum-sun-clock features the unusual double-reflected monogram of both rulers ("GP") under the crown.

RIGHT: POTSDAM CUP. G. HOSSAUER, AFTER A DESIGN BY F. SCHINKEL. BERLIN. 1830.
SILVER, CHASING, ENGRAVING, GILDING, ENAMEL, PAINTING. 28.5 X 22 X 35. INV. NO PDMP 20/1-4DM. Fashioned in the ornate style of Germany's celebrated medieval silversmiths, this intricately crafted cup was commissioned in honor of German-born Empress Alexandra Fyodorovna's birthday, celebrated at the new Prussian royal palace in Potsdam in 1829. It features coats-of-arms of each royal house represented at the event.

Palaces of St. Petersburg

These and following pages: Most celebrated for the series of exquisitely crafted and bejewelled Easter eggs which were commissioned by the Russian royal family, the St. Petersburg firm of Karl Fabergé in 1885 became the official "jeweler" for the Romanovs, supplying the luxury-minded Russian court with a staggering amount of precious objets d'art. Among thousands of such objects scattered throughout the imperial palaces of Russia, these examples in the collections of Peterhof were among the personal favorites of the royal family.

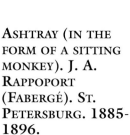

ASHTRAY (IN THE FORM OF A SITTING MONKEY). J. A. RAPPOPORT (FABERGÉ). ST. PETERSBURG. 1885-1896.
SILVER, CASTING, CHASING. 4.2 X 7.5. INV. NO. PDMP 333-DM.

CLOCK À LA LOUIS XVI. H. WIGSTROM (FABERGÉ). ST. PETERSBURG. 1896-1908.
SILVER, GOLD, RUBIES, ENAMEL. 20 X 9.5. INV. NO. PDMP 334-DM.

TABLE CLOCK. M. E. PERCHIN (FABERGÉ). ST. PETERSBURG. 1894-1896.
MARBLE, SILVER, CHASING, ENAMEL, STEEL, BURNISHING. HEIGHT-17.5. INV. NO. PDMP 501-MB.

GLUE BOTTLE. P. T. RINGE (FABERGÉ). ST. PETERSBURG. 1893.
QUARTZITE, NEPHRITE, GOLD, DIAMONDS. HEIGHT-7.0. INV. NO. PDMP 530-DM.

**BEAUTY-SPOT CASE.
H. WIGSTROM
(FABERGÉ). ST.
PETERSBURG. 1896-
1908.**
SILVER, TRANSPARENT
ENAMEL AGAINST GUIL-
LOCHE GROUND, GOLD.
1.5 X 13.5 X 1.5. INV.
NO PDMP 317-DM.

**LITTLE CUP. A. J.
NEVALAINEN
(FABERGÉ). ST.
PETERSBURG. 1896-
1908.**
SILVER, CHASING, GILD-
ING, ENAMEL ON GUIL-
LOCHE GROUND. HEIGHT-
3.7; DIAMETER-6. INV.
NO. PDMP 335-DM.

**MODEL OF THE
MONUMENT TO PETER
THE GREAT. J. A.
RAPPOPORT
(FABERGÉ), AFTER
"BRONZE
HORSEMAN" BY M.
FALCONET. ST.
PETERSBURG. 1890-
1903.**
MARBLE, SILVER, CARV-
ING, CHASING. INV. NO.
PDMP 1007-DM.

**GOBLET WITH
SITTING BEARS (ONE
OF TWO). FABERGÉ.
MOSCOW. 1890S.**
SILVER, CHASING, GILD-
ING. HEIGHT-9.7. INV.
NO. PDMP 661-DM.

PAPERWEIGHT (FROM THE STUDY OF MARIA FYODOROVNA). ST. PETERSBURG. 1880-1885.
LAPIS LAZULI, SILVER, CHASING, CARVING. 22.8 X 17.9 X 9.4. INV. NO. PDMP 58-DM.

VASE IN A CASE. FABERGÉ. MOSCOW. 1908-1917.
CUT CRYSTAL, CARVING, SILVER, CHASING, GILDING. HEIGHT-20.4. INV. NOS. PDMP 672-DM, 672/1-DM.

TROPHY CUP IN A CASE. J. A. RAPPOPORT (FABERGÉ). MOSCOW. 1898.

SILVER, GILDING, CHASING, ENGRAVING. HEIGHT OF THE CUP-39.7; CASE-19.8. INV. NOS. 656-DM, 656/1-DM.

Topped with the double-headed Romanov eagle and studded with medallions commemorating the reigns of Peter I to Nicholas II, this baroque-style trophy cup and case was presented to Counts Fyodor Gustavovich and Kyril Fyodorovich Berg, winners of the first "Tsar's Cup," at the Nevsky Yachting Club, on May 30, 1898.

WRITING SET OF EIGHT PIECES (INKSET, FEATHER CLEANER AND STAND, FOUR VASES, AND CASKET). RUSSIA. 1830-1840.

MALACHITE, BRONZE. INV. NOS. PDMP 2411-2415, 2435, 107-108.

SMALL CHEST. TULA, RUSSIA. 1710S.
STEEL, BRONZE.
27 X 24 X 19.
INV. NO. PDMP 2-MT.
Decorated with a plated monogram of Peter I and soldiers' masques in cocked hats, this early work from the new center of Russia's iron industry was perhaps a gift from Tula craftsmen to Peter the Great.

PAIR OF BUSTS OF TSAR ALEXANDER I AND EMPRESS ELIZABETH ALEXEEVNA. FRANCE. 1800S.
GILDED AND PATINATED BRONZE. HEIGHT-54.5.
INV. NOS. PDMP 176-177-MT.
These unmarked busts, perhaps a diplomatic gift from France, feature the monograms of the tsar and tsarina on the pedestals.

LEFT AND OPPOSITE:
Peter the Great's working
study in the Grand Palace
at Peterhof originally featured twelve carved-oak
wall panels designed as an
allegoric "anthem" to the
rebirth of science, cul-
ture, trade, and military
might ushered in by the
westward-thinking tsar.
Crafted in 1717-1720 by
Russian masters after
drawings by the French
sculptor Nicolas Pineau,
only six panels (three,
left) have survived today.
One panel, right, meticu-
lously re-created in 1983
by Peterhof restorers
from archival photos and
eighteenth-century docu-
ments, replaces one of
the six panels lost to the
Nazis in WWII.

**TABLE. HANNOVER,
GERMANY. 1700-
1730.**
OAK, WALNUT, INTARSIA.
72 X 104 X 66. INV. NO.
100-MB.

Palaces of St. Petersburg

LEFT: CORONATION
THRONE ARMCHAIR
OF TSAR NICHOLAS
II. FACTORY OF A.
SCHMIDT. MOSCOW.
1894.
BIRCH, CARVING, GILD-
ING, BRONZE, SILVER,
BROCADE, NEEDLEWORK.
182 X 93 X 91. INV. NO.
PDMP 993-MB.
Crafted for Nicholas II's
coronation in 1894, the
most recent of the
Russian imperial thrones
was constructed from
drawings prepared by the
curator of the Armory in
Moscow and borrows
heavily from designs from
the Byzantine church in
Salonika, Greece; St.
Mark's Cathedral in
Venice; and St. Simon's
Monastery in Moscow.
With embroidery display-
ing the monogram of
Nicholas II, the throne
chair now sits in the
Throne Hall of the
Grand Palace beneath a
celebrated painting of
Catherine the Great by
Vigilius Erichsen.

THE CORONATION
THRONE ARMCHAIR
OF EMPRESS MARIA
FYODOROVNA.
FACTORY OF LISERET
BROTHERS. ST.
PETERSBURG. 1856.
LINDEN, CARVING, GILD-
ING, PAINTING, BROCADE,
EMBROIDERY, APPLIQUÉ,
SILVER. 215 X 112.5 X
57.5. INV. NO. PDMP
1719.MB.

Originally prepared for
the Andreevsky Hall of
the Grand Kremlin Palace
in Moscow for the coro-
nation ceremony of
Alexander II and Maria
Alexandrovna in 1856,
the throne was renovated
twenty-six years later for
the coronation ceremony
of Alexander III and
Maria Fyodorovna.

STATUE "NYMPHE."
ST. PETERSBURG.
1856.
COPPER, GALVANOPLASTY,
GILDING. HEIGHT-156.
INV. NO. PDMP 235/1-
SK.
A copy of a Russian original in marble which now
stands in the Hermitage
Museum in St.
Petersburg (which, in
turn, was a replica of the
antique original of the
third century B.C.), this
sister statue to "Danaïde"
(opposite) sits in the east-
ern parterres of the
Lower Park.

RIGHT:
STATUE "DANAÏDE."
ST. PETERSBURG.
1853.
GILDED BRONZE.
HEIGHT-157.
Part of the fountain
ensemble by the same
name in the Lower Park,
the present "Danaïde" is
a gilded bronze replica of
a marble original com-
missioned by Nicholas I
and executed by the
German sculptor
Christian Daniel Rauch.
In ancient mythology one
of the daughters of the
king of Argos, Danaïde is
doomed for eternity to
fill a bottomless barrel,
here represented as a
large, classical urn.

BELOW: SADDLE OF CATHERINE THE GREAT'S HORSE "BRILLIANT." RUSSIA. MID-1700S.

VELVET, EMBROIDERY WITH GOLD, GALLOON, LEATHER, METAL, GILDING. 72 X 59. INV. NOS. 239-BK, 239/1-7-BK.

The saddle harness, decorated with crimson velvet and traditional Russian embroidery with gold, was manufactured during the reign of Peter the Great's daughter, Elizabeth, and witnessed the events of the June 28, 1762, palace coup, in which Catherine II returned with her guards to Peterhof to successfully overthrow her husband, Peter III. The saddle, one of the prize objects of the exhibition, is prominently featured in the painting of Catherine the Great by Vigilius Erichsen.

ABOVE, RIGHT AND OVERLEAF: BOOK: "THE DESCRIPTION OF THE HOLY CORONATION OF THEIR MAJESTIES TSAR ALEXANDER II AND THE EMPRESS MARIA ALEXANDROVNA." THE PRINTING HOUSE OF THE IMPERIAL ACADEMY OF SCIENCES. ST. PETERSBURG. 1856.

LEATHER, BRASS, GILDING; PAPER, CHROMOLITHOGRAPHY. 92 X 70 X 6. INV. NO. PDMP 206, 206/1-17-RK.

The largest book in all Russia, this weighty volume features a leather and brass-tooled cover stamped with the imperial standards and monograms of the tsar and tsarina and contains color lithographs of watercolors expertly reproduced in Paris at the house of J.R. Lemercier. Two of the seventeen scenes depicting the coronation ceremony shown here include the solemn "Annointing of His Majesty the Tsar" (opposite) and "(Handing Out of the Leaflet) Announcing the Coronation on Red Square" (following pages).

PAIR OF TILSIT VASES (FRONT AND BACK VIEWS). ROYAL PORCELAIN MANUFACTORY. SEVRES, FRANCE. 1807.

PORCELAIN, UNDERGLAZE COBALT COVERING, OVERGLAZE GRISAILLE PAINTING, GOLD PAINTING; BRONZE, GILDING. HEIGHT-55. INV. NOS. PDMP 1255,1256-F.

A diplomatic gift from Napoleon to Alexander I after the tsar recognized the French emperor's "redrawing" of Europe at the negotiations at Tilsit in 1807, these rare treasures from Peterhof's collection of objets d'art feature replicas of illustrations from a celebrated French edition of the poetry of Virgil. The detail (opposite) shows a shepherd of Arcadia, a scene from the poet's "Bucolica." They presently adorn the mantel of the Drawing Room of the "Cottage Palace."

THE CLOCK "ROUEN
CATHEDRAL" AND
TWO CANDELABRA.
CLOCK—MODEL BY P.
VAKHRAMEEV, PAINT-
ING BY N. YAKOVLEV;
CANDELABRA—
UNMARKED. IMPERIAL
PORCELAIN WORKS.
ST. PETERSBURG.
1830.
PORCELAIN, OVERGLAZE
POLYCHROME PAINTING,
GOLD PAINTING; BRONZE,
GILDING. HEIGHT

(CLOCK)-86; (CANDE-
LABRA)-70. INV. NO.
PDMP 1508-F.

Gracing the mantel of the
Drawing Room of the
Cottage Palace, the
cathedral-shaped clock
with "rose window" face
and appropriately ornate
candelabra were executed
in a neo-Gothic style in
keeping with the
nineteenth-century decor
of the room.

Palaces of St. Petersburg

Navy Uniform Dress of Catherine the Great. St. Petersburg. 1796.
Silk, embroidery with gold; copper, gilding. Instituted by Catherine II as the ladies' equivalent of dress uniforms, designs such as this combined the distinguishing marks of the uniforms of various regiments (color of fabric, galloons, buttons) with the elements of traditional Russian ladies' dresses (flap sleeves, gold lace) and modern European costumes of the time (hoops, pleating, etc.). On display in the Portrait Gallery of the Grand Palace, Catherine would have worn this example to receive officers of her navy.

Pair of Vases. Imperial Glass Works. St. Petersburg. 1820s.
Two-layer ruby-colored glass, carving; bronze, chasing, gilding. Height-24. Length-23.8. Inv. nos. PDMP 2244-2245-st. Adorning a tabletop in the Catherine Pavilion, these gem-colored treasures in the form of horns-of-plenty attest to the refinement of the Russian glassmaker's craft.

Palaces of St. Petersburg

Catherine Palace

The Catherine Palace occupies a special place among the architectural monuments of Russia. It is easy to understand the secret of its charm: its grandeur is both solemn and exuberant at the same time. In the dim light of the northern sun, the brilliant azure walls, snow-white columns, gold sculpture, and glittering onion-shaped domes create a fairyland setting. More importantly, the Catherine Palace represents a whole epoch in Russian history.

For three centuries, the palace served as the chief residence of the Russian monarchs. Starting with Peter the Great at the beginning of the eighteenth century, the Romanov tsars and tsarinas lived, worked, and entertained in its splendid rooms and halls. Besides its historical significance, the palace has an enormous importance as a creation of art. A uniquely Russian phenomenon, the palace compound has absorbed all the best of all the other cultures of Europe, the whole synthesized into a singularly dramatic Russian vernacular. Beginning in 1718, celebrated architects such as Bartolomeo Rastrelli, Charles Cameron, Giacomo Quarenghi, and Ippolit Monigetti worked on different parts of it. Several generations of native and foreign painters, sculptors, carvers, and other craftsmen worked here, as well. By the mid-eighteenth century, the scale of the palace construction works in Saint Petersburg, the relatively new capital of the empire, was the largest in all Europe.

Re-created for the exhibition, Bartolomeo Rastrelli's magnificent Portrait Hall at the Catherine Palace boasts two "Dutch" tiled stoves and an intricate parquet floor refurbished by contemporary masters after the original 1765 design.

The idea for a new palace had begun in 1710, when Peter the Great presented his wife, Catherine I, with a small estate, which was later named "Tsarskoje Selo" ("Tsar's Village"). Seven years later, a decision was made to turn the property into the official imperial summer residence. It was then that construction began on a stone palace, built at the top of a hill on the estate. Later, service buildings—stables, carriage houses, workmen's quarters, and so forth—were sited in a straight axis running from the front of the palace, an avenue that later formed the main street of the "royal village." The construction of a small wooden church and a formal garden completed the first phase of the property's development. West of the palace, a small section of forest land was fenced off to house game for the tsar's hunt.

The period of the reign of the cultured daughter of Peter I, Elizabeth Petrovna (1741-1762), was perhaps the most fruitful for the palace and park ensemble at

Tsarskoje Selo. Elizabeth spared neither manpower nor financial resources for building projects at her favorite residence. Soon after her ascension to the throne, she ordered the construction of two colonnaded galleries and stone "pavilions," which would fan out from the main palace. In 1752, she hired the brilliant Italian architect, Bartolomeo Rastrelli, who designed three more buildings—the Hermitage, Grotto, and Monbijou Pavilions. These jewel-like edifices served as elegant counterpoints to the ever-expanding series of formal gardens which surrounded the Catherine Palace. Characterized by the solemn, monumental ornateness of the Russian baroque style, his additions to the complex at Tsarskoje Selo dazzled his contemporaries with the splendor and endless fantasy of their designs. Moreover, he redesigned and refurbished much of the original palace, making walls higher and redecorating facades. The most impressive additions to the facades were the figures of Atlas—seventy in all—which delineated the exteriors of the palace. The impression of grandeur was further intensified by the addition of gilded wooden sculptures and vases to the roof—magnificent decorative elements which, unfortunately, have not survived to the present day.

This abundant gilding of architectural and sculptural details on the facade was matched by plenty of gold in the interiors. Incredibly, more than one hundred kilograms of gold were used for the decoration. Despite this emphasis on "plastic" decorative elements, the distinguishing feature of the Catherine Palace remained its simplicity and lucidity of composition. Geometrically straightforward, the interiors essentially comprise one huge suite of rooms layed out in a straight line, giving a dramatic impression of endless space. Contemporaries called this formal suite, beginning at the Grand Staircase and ending at the chapel, the "Golden Enfilade." Among the spectacular wood-carved and gilded rooms of particular note running along this axis are a series of five Anterooms, intended for receptions with the empress; a Grand Hall (the "Gallery"); the Chinese Suite, with its rare Oriental porcelains; the gem-like Amber Room; and the stunning Portrait Hall, with walls covered with canvases by the likes of Luca Giordano, Emmanuel de Witte, Adrian van Ostade, and other masters of the leading European schools of the seventeenth and eighteenth centuries. The over-decoration of the four doors of this hall are considered the most magnificent in the whole palace. Large sculptured caryatids and images of Minerva and the cupids lend a Greco-Roman majesty to the room's decor.

In the Portrait Hall, as well as the other principal rooms, plafond (ceiling) paintings, executed by talented Italian masters imported to the Russian court, depict popular subjects from classical mythology and glorify the reign of Elizabeth Petrovna. And the parquet floors, intricately fashioned in a variety of rare woods, have no less significance than the paintings and gilded decoration of the walls.

By the 1770s, a new luxury-minded proprietress, Catherine the Great, began yet another phase of construction at Tsarskoje Selo. Upon her ascension to the throne, she immediately had the gilded statues and vases removed from the palace's roof and the gilded figures of Atlas on the facade stripped and painted a more discreet yellow. The Grand Staircase was transferred from the southern wing to the center of the palace, and the pavilions connected to the main building were enlarged.

Beginning in 1779, the Scottish architect, Charles Cameron, was entrusted with refurbishing the interior decoration of the palace. Cameron, like Giacomo Quarenghi, who was to arrive later, was a passionate admirer of all things "antique." Both architects were at the vanguard of a new movement in the art of the late eighteenth century—classicism—and both tried to express the ideals of beauty by the strict proportions of classical art. As opposed to Rastrelli's work, Cameron's rooms, including the private apartments of Catherine the Great and the exquisite Blue Formal Drawing Room, are marked by the simplicity of their proportions, a restrained color palette, and the cool elegance of their decorative elements. Although Quarenghi refurbished only two interiors of the palace—the Mirror and Silver Studies of Catherine II—he designed the Alexandrovsky Palace in 1796 for the eldest grandson of Catherine, Alexander II. Nicholas II, the last Russian tsar, spent his last years in this palace, and it was from here that the imperial family was exiled to the Urals during the revolution of 1917.

OVERLEAF: Scottish architect Charles Cameron imbued the lovely Blue Formal Drawing Room with references to classical antiquity, such as the frescoed ceiling and medallions imbedded in the cornices. Considered quite avant-garde when he designed it, the room has been meticulously re-created for the present exhibition.

After the October Revolution of that year, the former imperial residence at Tsarskoye Selo was transformed into a museum, and the Catherine Palace was opened for visitors on June 9, 1918. During the Second World War, Tsarskoje Selo (which had been renamed "Pushkin" in 1937) was occupied by the German Nazis for twenty-eight months. Their regiments were quartered in the halls of the palace, which also housed garages and ammunition depots. Many objects of art (including all of the mosaic panels of the Amber Room) were stolen or lost forever.

The restoration works at the palace began only in 1957. The refurbishment of each interior required an enormous amount of work by the best craftsmen and the meticulous study of a number of historical documents—not to mention a colossal amount of money. At present, twenty-three of the fifty-five formal rooms at the Catherine Palace have been restored, and the works are still going on.

—*Galina Khodasevich*

The interior of the Portrait Hall, part of the formal suite of rooms at the Catherine Palace known as the "Golden Enfilade," was created in the eighteenth century by the Italian master Bartolomeo Rastrelli. Utilized chiefly for the receptions of foreign ambassadors and other dignitaries, it was also the room where the royal family reposed, played chess and checkers with their retainers, and conversed with court ladies and cavaliers.

The walls of the hall are upholstered in a precious white damask enframed with elegant, gilded rococo ornament, and state portraits of the Russian tsarinas line the walls. For the ceiling, Nicholas I in 1855 commissioned a large painting, which was later tragically lost during WWII. During the re-creation of the interior in 1980, a plafond painting by the Italian master, Giovanni Tiepolo, was mounted into the ceiling. Featuring a complicated perspective, the oval-shaped work depicts an illusion of open sky surrounded by mythological figures, including Mercury, Glory, and the other denizens of Mount Olympus seated dramatically on an eagle. Figures symbolizing the continents are depicted together with Neptune, who brandishes an oversized oar. The dynamic composition, with its contrast of colors—red, yellow, blue, and green—lends an air of festivity to a room otherwise dominated by the stateliness of the portraits. Complementing the dramatic ambiance imparted by Tiepolo's work, the decoration of the doors and two large mirrors point up Rastrelli's vivid imagination. Gilded carving, in the form of a fabulous wreath of floral garlands interwoven with stems and leaves, appears to grow around the frames of the mirrors. Likewise, the portals of the doors are decorated with gilded figures of cupids, the whole appearing to grow as if it were some kind of fantastic tree. The sculpture of the cupids' heads is so realistic that the faces actually appear to be alive.

By 1982, after many years of monotonous, labor-intensive work, the Portrait Hall once again began to acquire its original appearance. Many of the portraits that had been evacuated during the Second World War were returned, and what was left of the furniture was painstakingly reupholstered and put back in its rightful place. The architectural decoration was refurbished with the help of archive documents, parts of the carvings that had been miraculously saved, and old photographs. The re-creation of the carving and the weaving of the white damask that had covered the walls and furniture was the most complicated task. During the process, the master carver Vladimir Slyozin discovered the ancient method of polishing gilded surfaces, and the carvings themselves were re-created by a team of contemporary masters. For a long time, it seemed impossible to find a method of weaving a white damask with such a complicated pattern as the original. Hundreds of samples of European fabrics from the eighteenth century were thoroughly studied. Finally it was decided to actually re-create an eighteenth-century weaving machine. The lost silk was then miraculously rewoven · using the same technique the original weavers had employed. Thanks to this kind of ingenuity, the Portrait Hall once again astonishes visitors by its magnificence.

—*T.F. Boulgakova*

BLUE FORMAL DRAWING ROOM

The exquisite Blue Formal Drawing Room was created at the end of the eighteenth century by the Scottish architect Charles Cameron, the celebrated connoisseur of classical architecture, for Grand Duke Paul Petrovich (1754-1801), the son of Catherine the Great and heir to the Russian throne.

At Tsarskoje Selo, Cameron was given carte blanche (not to mention the wherewithal) to fully realize the classical ideals he had formulated after years of studying the art and architecture of ancient Greece and Rome. The Blue Formal Drawing Room, perhaps Cameron's masterpiece at the Catherine Palace, is the largest and smartest room of the apartments of the Grand Duke. Distinguished by the richness and variety of its decoration, the room gets its name from walls upholstered with sumptuous white silk with delicately painted blue flowers, the whole enframed with carved and gilded ornamentation. The suite of armchairs designed by Cameron is upholstered with the same silk. The ceiling friezes are decorated with gilded moldings, and eighty oval medallions boast paintings on a variety of mythological subjects, such as cupids and griffins, the latter of which have become the logo for the present exhibition. The pattern of the ceiling harmonizes with that of the inlaid floor, which is executed in a variety of precious woods. The light-shaded palm, rosewood, linden, and walnut elegantly contrast with the darker tones of palisander, mahogany, ebony, and amaranth. The skillfully laid parquet pattern is further embellished with engraved flowers. On the walls hang the portraits of Tsarskoje Selo's former proprietors: Peter the Great, his wife Catherine I, their daughter Elizabeth Petrovna, Catherine II, her son Paul Petrovich, and his wife, Maria Fyodorovna.

During WWII, the northern wing of the palace, where the Blue Formal Drawing Room is situated, suffered less than many of the other interiors. Nevertheless, the silk upholstery of the walls, the ceiling painting and medallions, and much of the sculptural decoration of the doors and cornices were either stolen or destroyed by the Nazis. But since there was no fire in the northern section of the palace, the magnificent parquet floor was relatively unscathed. After years of research and millions of rubles, the silk upholstery of the walls has been re-created to match surviving samples housed at the Silk Research Institute in Moscow. Painters and gilders restored the ceiling frieze, and sculptors worked tirelessly to refurbish door portals, fireplaces, and cornices. Much of the room's furnishings and paintings had been evacuated to Siberia, and all of it eventually was returned safely.

The Blue Formal Drawing Room, among the first rooms of the Catherine Palace to be restored, was opened again in 1959. Almost forty years later, this marvelous interior created by Cameron two hundred years ago continues to amaze visitors from around the world.

—*T.M. Boutyrina*

IVAN NICOLAEVICH ADOLSKY. PORTRAIT OF EMPRESS CATHERINE I. 1725-1726.
OIL ON CANVAS. 2,230 X 1,400. INV. NO. 757-X. Set in an ornate frame executed by master carver Jean-Baptiste Sharleman, this imposing likeness of Peter the Great's wife presently hangs in the Portrait Hall of the Catherine Palace.

All of the fireplace accessories in the Blue Formal Drawing Room, including the fire tongs (left) and the fireplace grid (above), were crafted in St. Petersburg after original designs by Charles Cameron.

LEFT AND RIGHT:
A novelty at the time, these white Italian marble fireplaces in the Blue Formal Drawing Room were designed in the 1780s by Charles Cameron to replace the traditional tiled stoves that are used elsewhere in the palace. Fitted with mirrors that reflect the sumptuous decor, the fireplaces are decorated with caryatids and carved friezes in the neo-classical style.

ANDIRONS. DESIGN BY CHARLES CAMERON. ST. PETERSBURG. 1783-1785.
GILDED BRONZE. HEIGHT-53. LENGTH-119. WIDTH-29. INV. NO. 44-IV.
Originally joined by gilded bronze rods, these Cameron-designed andirons feature sphynxes resting on ornamented pedestals.

Palaces of St. Petersburg

83

LEFT:
CLOCK. GALLIEN LEROY. PARIS. 1750-1800.
GILDED BRONZE, MARBLE. HEIGHT-51. LENGTH-62. WIDTH-17. INV. NO. 222-IV.
In keeping with the "antique" theme of the Blue Formal Drawing Room's frescoed ceiling and cornice decorations, this timepiece is a whimsical tribute to Bacchus, here attended by a satyr (front) and Momus (rear), the Greek god of laughter.

RIGHT:
CLOCK. WORKSHOP OF DEVERBERIE. PARIS. LATE 1700s.
GILDED AND PATINATED BRONZE. HEIGHT-53. LENGTH-57. WIDTH-14. INV. NO. 122-IV.
Part of a series entitled *"Pendule au bon negre,"* this French masterwork lends an exotic touch to the neo-classical formality of the Blue Formal Drawing Room.

LEFT: CANDELABRUM (ONE OF A PAIR). ST. PETERSBURG. NINETEENTH CENTURY.
GILDED BRONZE, MARBLE. HEIGHT-1,237. INV. NO. 1165-IV.
Designed after a French model of the late eighteenth century, this neoclassical bronze masterwork alludes to classical antiquity with the figures of water nymphs beneath the stem and griffins on its base.

ABOVE AND FOLLOWING PAGE: CANDELABRA (TWO OF EIGHT). WORKSHOP OF PIERRE-PHILIPPE THOMIRE. PARIS. 1790s.
GILDED BRONZE, MARBLE. HEIGHT-84. LENGTH-25. INV. NOS. 1199-1202-IV.
Part of the over-mantle decor of the two fireplaces in the Blue Formal Drawing Room, these candelabra, each in the form of "Victory" holding a vase, perfectly complement the rest of the mantel's classically themed garniture.

ABOVE, CENTER:
VASE "THE DECREE
ON PROVINCES."
IMPERIAL PORCELAIN
WORKS. ST.
PETERSBURG. 1770S.
PORCELAIN. HEIGHT-
46.5. INV. NO. 729-I.
Crowned with a gilded
pinecone and featuring
an allegorical depiction of
Catherine the Great in
the guise of Minerva, this
gilded and painted vase
rests on a mantel in the
Blue Formal Drawing
Room and is flanked by
two porcelain vases from
Germany.

RIGHT:
VASE (ONE OF A PAIR).
FRANCE. 1825-1850.
PORCELAIN, GILDING,
PAINTING, TOOLING.
HEIGHT-49. INV. NO.
2830-I.
One of a pair of gilded
vases gracing the ends of
a mantel in the Blue
Formal Drawing Room,
this Empire-style example
borrows the theme of its
painted medallions from
Jean de la Fontaine's
story "The Love of
Psyche and Cupid."

HEINRICH
BUCHHOLTZ.
PORTRAIT OF EMPRESS
ELIZABETH
PETROVNA. 1768.
OIL ON CANVAS. 2,600 X
2,000. INV. NO. 761-X.
For unknown reasons,
the face in this painting is
not the original, a fact
that was not discovered
until 1918. Set in a frame
that matches that of the
portrait on page 81, the
painting was commis-
sioned by Catherine the
Great.

LEFT:
IVAN N. NIKITIN.
PORTRAIT OF PETER
THE GREAT IN NAVAL
BATTLE SCENE. 1715.
OIL ON CANVAS. 152 X
108. INV. NO. 755-X.
Nikitin was one of Peter
the Great's favorite
painters, and this canvas,
which hangs in the Blue
Formal Drawing Room,
represents one of the ear-
liest examples of a dis-
tinctly Russian school of
portrait painting.

RIGHT:
PORTRAIT OF EMPRESS
CATHERINE I.
UNKNOWN PAINTER,
RUSSIAN SCHOOL.
NINETEENTH-CENTU-
RY REPLICA OF AN
EIGHTEENTH-CENTU-
RY ORIGINAL BY JEAN-
MARC NATTIER.
OIL ON CANVAS. 152 X
108. INV. NO. 758-X.
An extremely popular
likeness of Peter the
Great's wife, Nattier's
original was copied by
numerous painters and
miniatures artists. This
replica now hangs in the
Blue Formal Drawing
Room.

TOP:
PORTRAIT OF THE GRAND DUCHESS NATALIA ALEXEEVNA. UNKNOWN PAINTER. NOT LATER THAN 1716.
OIL ON CANVAS.
INV. NO. 985-X.
This replica of an original perhaps executed by the court painter Ivan Nikitin depicts Peter the Great's favorite sister, one of the most educated Russian women of her time. It now hangs in the Portrait Hall of the Catherine Palace.

BOTTOM:
PORTRAIT OF EMPRESS CATHERINE II. UNKNOWN PAINTER. LATE 1700s.
OIL ON CANVAS.
INV. NO. 776-X.
One of many popular replicas of an unknown eighteenth-century original, this canvas was purchased by Nicholas II in 1909 and has been exhibited in the Portrait Hall of the Catherine Palace since 1982.

VIGILIUS ERICHSEN. PORTRAIT OF EMPRESS ELIZABETH PETROVNA. 1758.
OIL ON CANVAS.
INV. NO. 762-X.
One of the most masterly of the formal portraits of the luxury-minded but politically shrewd tsarina, this canvas by the popular court painter has always been in the collection of the Catherine Palace, except for its evacuation during WWII.

LEFT:
**PORTRAIT OF THE
GRAND DUCHESS
MARIA FYODOROVNA.
UNKNOWN PAINTER.
RUSSIA. EARLY
1800s.**
OIL ON CANVAS.
INV. NO. 779-X.
The jewel-toned colors of
the grand duchess's robe
and sash are an arresting
counterpoint to the soft,
feminine beauty of the
future tsarina. A replica
of an earlier painting by
the French artist M. L. E.
Viger-Lebrun, the por-
trait hangs in the Blue
Formal Drawing Room.

RIGHT:
**ALEXANDER ROSLIN.
PORTRAIT OF THE
GRAND DUKE PAUL
PETROVICH. 1777.**
OIL ON CANVAS.
INV. NO. 777-X.
A distinguished member
of the "Academie" in
Paris and the Art
Academy of his native
Stockholm, the artist exe-
cuted a number of popu-
lar paintings for the
imperial court of Russia,
including this elegant —
and true-to-life — like-
ness of Catherine the
Great's oldest son and
heir.

PLAFOND PAINTING. THE MEETING OF ANTHONY AND CLEOPATRA. UNKNOWN PAINTER. 1700-1750.

OIL ON CANVAS. INV. NO. 983-X.

One of a number of paintings commissioned for the ceilings of the various imperial residences near St. Petersburg, this example survived the destruction of WWII and has been installed in the Portrait Hall ceiling of the present exhibition as a substitution for the original at the Catherine Palace.

RIGHT:
TABLE WITH LIFTING SCREEN TOP. UNKNOWN MASTER. TULA, RUSSIA. 1780S.
STEEL, GILDED BRONZE, GLASS; POLISHING, BURNISHING, SILVER AND GOLD INLAID PATTERNS, FACETING, CHASING. 59 X 41 X 79. INV. NO. 25-V. The center of armory production in Russia since the sixteenth century, Tula had become more celebrated by the mid-eighteenth century for its innovative use of steel in the manufacture of furniture and decorative objects. The skillful use of steel faceting, gold and silver inlay, and glass etching gives this table a refinement more closely associated with the jeweller's craft than that of the cabinetmaker's.

CYLINDER-TOP BUREAU. MATVEI YAKOVLEVICH VERETENNIKOV. ST. PETERSBURG. BEFORE 1796.
MAPLE, STAINED MAPLE, BOX-TREE, WALNUT, PLANE-TREE, EBONY, ROSEWOOD, APPLE-TREE, PALISANDER, GILDED BRONZE, MOTHER-OF-PEARL, MOROCCO; MARQUETRY, INCRUSTATION, ENGRAVING, LACQUERING. 127 X 84 X 161. INV. NO. 135-V.

One of the finest examples of the eighteenth-century Russian *ébeniste*'s craft, this bureau was personally commissioned by Catherine the Great following her 1787 trip to the newly annexed Crimea. With masterfully executed inlaid scenes of the empress accepting the keys to Constantinople, the desk represents Catherine's lifelong dream of restoring the Byzantine Empire.

RIGHT:
CONSOLE (ONE OF A PAIR). AFTER ORIGINALS DESIGNED BY CHARLES CAMERON AND EXECUTED BY JEAN-BAPTISTE SHARLEMAN. LENINGRAD. 1950S.
WOOD, MARBLE; CARVING, GILDING, PAINTING. 130 X 65 X 83. INV. NO. 491-V.
An example of the peerless expertise of the contemporary Russian restorer's art, this marble-topped console was recreated for the Blue Formal Drawing Room using photos and eighteenth-century archive documents.

OVERLEAF:
The spectacular ceiling of the Blue Formal Drawing Room, fashioned by Charles Cameron in the style of the frescoes of ancient Pompeii, depicts mythological scenes and features the signature griffins of the present exhibition. With a bow to classical order, the pattern of the ceiling harmonizes perfectly with that of the inlaid parquet floor.

ARMCHAIR (ONE OF FOUR). JEAN-BAPTISTE SHARLEMAN, AFTER A DESIGN BY CHARLES CAMERON. ST. PETERSBURG. 1783.
WOOD, SILK; CARVING, GILDING. 81 X 64 X 111. INV. NO. 112-V.
Although most of Cameron's funiture for the Blue Formal Drawing Room was lost during WWII, this superb example of his early neo-classical style was expertly restored and re-upholstered in silk painstakingly re-created after the eighteenth-century original.

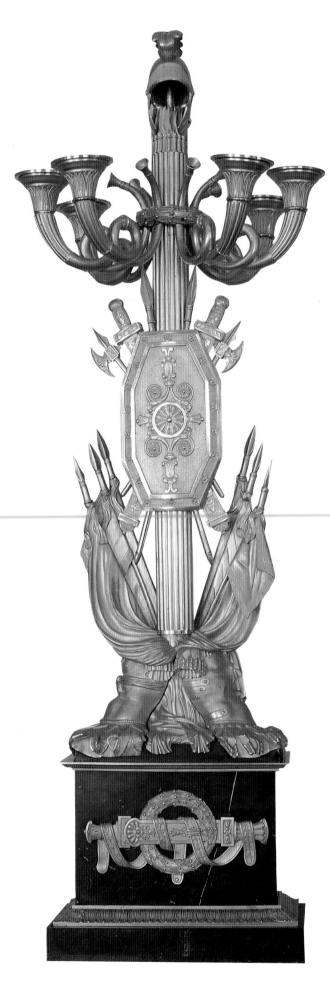

Palaces of St. Petersburg

Palaces of St. Petersburg

VASE. IMPERIAL PORCELAIN WORKS. ST. PETERSBURG. 1780S.
PORCELAIN. HEIGHT-135. WIDTH-57. DIAMETER-46.5. INV. NO. 728-I. Unusual for its large dimensions, this gift to Catherine the Great features the tsarina's bas-relief profiles and her monogram ("EII," for Ekaterina II) fashioned as handles.

RIGHT: CLOCK "PEACE AND PLENTY." JEAN-LOUIS PRIERE, AFTER THE DRAWING BY FRANÇOIS BOUCHER. MECHANISM BY ANTOINE PELTIER. FRANCE. 1770.
GILDED AND PATINATED BRONZE. 102 X 76. INV. NO. 1168-IV. Commissioned for the study of the future Louis XVI at Versailles, this French masterpiece was originally embellished with the Bourbon fleur-de-lis and a royal crown, both of which were removed after the French Revolution. Eventually sold to the Russian court and housed in both the Winter and Catherine Palaces, it was earmarked for sale abroad after the 1917 revolution but miraculously survived in a storage vault in Moscow. In 1971, the clock was finally returned to the Catherine Palace.

Palaces of St. Petersburg

RELIQUARY. ST. PETERSBURG. C. 1767.
SILVER, GILDING. HEIGHT-75. LENGTH-29. WIDTH-26. INV. NO. 744-IV.
A traditional Russian Orthodox holy vessel that would have contained the Communion bread and sacrament wine, this decidedly royal example originally graced an altar in one of the chapels at Tsarskoje Selo.

Palaces of St. Petersburg

VASE-CANDELABRUM. ROYAL PORCELAIN MANUFACTORY. BERLIN. 1824.

PORCELAIN, GOLD PAINTING, BRONZE, PATINATED BRONZE, CHASED ORMOLU. HEIGHT-132. HEIGHT OF THE VASE-81.5. DIAMETER-53. INV. NOS. 1815-IV, 1815/I-IV.

Featuring miniature replicas of Raphael's *Triumph of Galatea* and Dufresnoy's *Coloration of the White Rose*, this painted and gilded Empire-period vase from Prussia was ingeniously outfitted with a "bouquet" of sixteen candle-holders by a St. Petersburg workshop in the mid-nineteenth century.

CASE FOR CHESS AND BACKGAMMON. GDANSK, POLAND. EARLY 1700s.
AMBER, WOOD, METAL. HEIGHT-12.5. LENGTH-46. WIDTH-43. INV. NO. 54-VI.

LEFT:
ON-TABLE CHEST OF DRAWERS. GDANSK, POLAND. 1700-1750.
AMBER, WOOD, METAL. HEIGHT-30.5. LENGTH-55. WIDTH-34. INV. NO. 61-VI.
One of the few original pieces of furniture from the Catherine Palace to have survived intact from the eighteenth century, this Polish chest decorated with Florentine-style mosaics is noted in the Palace's inventory of 1765.

NEAR RIGHT:
ON-TABLE DECORATION (SHELL WITH PUTTI). KASSEL, GERMANY. 1700-1750.
OPAQUE AMBER. HEIGHT-4.2. LENGTH-12.6. WIDTH-7.5. INV. NO. 8-VI.

MIDDLE RIGHT:
SMALL BOX. GDANSK, POLAND. 1690-1710.
AMBER. HEIGHT-3.5. DIAMETER-7.9. INV. NO. 123-VI.

NEAR LEFT:
CASKET-NECESSAIRE. GDANSK, POLAND. 1690-1710.
AMBER, WOOD, METAL, VELVET, MIRROR GLASS. HEIGHT-16. LENGTH-13.7. WIDTH-13.4. INV. NO. 59-VI.
This early combination sewing and manicure kit would have originally contained an amber shuttle, needlecase, small knife, thimbles, and a perfume bottle.

Palaces of St. Petersburg

THIS PAGE, TOP AND BOTTOM: SCONCE (ONE OF A PAIR) AND CONSOLE TABLE (DETAIL). DESIGN BY IPPOLIT ANTONOVICH MONIGETTI. ST. PETERSBURG. 1860S. LAPIS LAZULI, GILDED BRONZE. SCONCE: HEIGHT-60; WIDTH-32. CONSOLE: HEIGHT-83; LENGTH-98; WIDTH-62. INV. NOS. 151-IV, 138-IV. Part of the sumptuous garniture of rare Badakhshin and Siberian lapis lazuli and gilded bronze designed for the Lyons Hall of the Catherine Palace, these pieces were among those commissioned by Empress Maria Alexandrovna in the 1860s in a style singularly Russian in its extravagance.

OVERLEAF:

One of the few complete collections of furniture and objects to have survived intact until the present day, the lapis lazuli garniture designed by Ippolit Monigetti for the Lyons Hall of the Catherine Palace represents a hallmark in the luxuriousness of nineteenth-century Russian design. The richly crafted pieces include pairs of consoles, secretaires, tables, cachepots, firescreens, and jardinieres, as well as a number of vases, sconces, candelabra, a barometer-thermometer, and a chandelier.

BREAKFAST TRAVELLING SET. ST. PETERSBURG. MID-1700s.
GILDED SILVER; GLASS. INV. NOS. 701-709-IV. This elegant rococo ensemble commissioned for Empress Elizabeth Petrovna includes eight pieces in a finely tooled leather case: a wine glass, table knife, two forks, tablespoon, teaspoon (with "flute" handle), eggcup, and a salt cellar with legs in the form of sharp-clawed paws.

RIGHT: TRAVELLING PISTOL SET. N. BOUTER. VERSAILLES ARMORY WORKS. VERSAILLES, FRANCE. EARLY 1800s.
INV. NO. 244/I-22. Walnut, mahogany, ebony, bone, horn, steel, and leather are some of the finely wrought materials used for this gun set, presented by Napoleon to Tsar Alexander I at Tilsit in 1807. An ironically appropriate gift (Napoleon would attack Russia five years later), the kit includes four pistols, as well as an assortment of tools for their maintenance.

THIS PAGE AND
RIGHT:
COLONEL'S UNIFORM
OF HIS MAJESTY'S
HUSSAR REGIMENT.
ST. PETERSBURG.
1890s.

Awarded the military rank of "colonel-for-life" by his father, an honor of which Nicholas II was unduly proud, it was fitting that he be married (1894) in the uniform of the prestigious Hussar Regiment. Restored in 1993, the complete outfit includes a scarlet cloth coat featuring gold shoulder braiding with a double-crowned monogram ("A II, III"), black patent-leather boots with spurs, a scarlet cap with a black patent-leather peak, and an officer's bag of red Morocco.

Palaces of St. Petersburg

CORONATION CARRIAGE. WORKSHOP OF TAZKI. ST. PETERSBURG. 1856.
GILDED WOOD AND BRONZE, LEATHER, CRYSTAL GLASS, VELVET, GOLD LACE. LENGTH-5M. WIDTH-2.4M. HEIGHT-2.95M. INV. NO. 294-VII. Decorated in an appropriately festive rococo style, this carriage was prepared especially for the 1856 coronation ceremonies of Alexander II in Moscow. Damaged by an exploding missile during WWII, it was restored by expert craftsmen from the Catherine Palace's restoration workshop in 1990.

Gatchina

The village of Gatchina, situated twenty-five miles south of St. Petersburg, was much older than the relatively new capital of the Russian Empire, having been mentioned in chronicles as early as 1499. However, it was not until the mid-eighteenth century, long after the other imperial palaces at Peterhof and Tsarskoje Selo had been built, that Gatchina began to acquire worldwide fame as the site of a palace which Catherine the Great had commissioned to be constructed for her lover and court favorite, Count Grigori Orlov.

It was Orlov, whom Catherine II once called "my angel, my dear precious husband, my fair golden pheasant," who had organized the palace coup that led to the assassination of Peter III in June of 1762 and to Catherine's ascension to the throne. Without Orlov, the rather insignificant German princess, born Sophia of Anhalt-Zerbst, might never have become Catherine "the Great," one of the most celebrated and controversial of Russia's monarchs.

Beginning in 1766, the construction of the palace at Gatchina, personally overseen by Catherine and inspired by the empress's voluminous correspondence with Voltaire, lasted until 1772, with the interiors completed by 1777. The whole enterprise was supervised by the Italian architect Antonio Rinaldi (1709-1794), whose main directive was to create a country house of a new kind, one which would forego the gilded grandeur of the palaces of earlier periods in favor of a refined simplicity that would harmonize with the natural parkland setting of the estate. It is no accident that the main facade of the palace is turned to the park, with two high, pentagonal towers anchoring the corners of the central structure and offering views from the palace down gently sloping lawns to the arcadian setting surrounding "Silver Lake." In contrast, the facade facing the village was decidedly less interesting. The whole complex was eventually made more elegant by Rinaldi's additions of two semicircular wings—decked out with graceful balconies—that fanned out from the central, rectangular block.

Inside, the main feature of the palace's decor was the restraint used in the selection of decorative materials—including a complete absence of gilding! Instead, subtle ornamentation on walls, archways, and ceilings counterbalanced the highly decorative elegance of splendid, intricately inlaid floors—the whole achieving a classical unity that

Originally the country estate of Catherine the Great's lover, Count Grigori Orlov, Gatchina had expanded into a full-blown royal palace by the time Semyon Shedrin painted the canvas *View of Gatchina Palace and Park*, a detail of which is shown here.

was quite avant-garde in an era decidedly fond of rococo exuberance.

Ironically, after Orlov's death in 1783, Catherine purchased the property from his heirs and gave it to her eldest son, Paul Petrovich, whose father had been murdered thanks to the crafty count. The grand duke detested his mother's role in his father's death, and, although it eventually became his favorite residence, the palace at Gatchina was at first something of a prison for him. Yet, it was at Gatchina that the talented and diligent tsarevich began to organize—in miniature—the future of Russia, an empire he felt should be managed along the principles of patriotism, the order of law, and extreme economy in spending money. The palace was soon transformed into its own little state, run along the lines of strict military discipline.

According to the tastes of its new owner (who was a true connoisseur of art, as well), it was decorated with the finest furniture and objets d'art in the new neo-classical style. While the exterior of the palace was refigured somewhat to suit the military turn of mind of its new proprietor (feudal-looking stone bastions were built and moats dug), inside, the central block was outfitted in an appropriately grand style by Vincenzo Brenna (1745-1820), who imbued the Marble Dining Room, Crimson Drawing Room, State Bedroom, and Throne Room with a solemn luxury befitting a monarch-to-be with absolutist tendencies.

After Paul I's ascension to the throne in 1796, these state rooms became the sites of gorgeous palace ceremonies, diplomatic receptions, formal dinners, balls, and so forth. In 1797, sessions of the Duma—the highest legislative body in the country—were first held at the palace. Because the residence was now deemed too small for such official functions, the main palace was continually enlarged throughout Paul's short reign.

On March 11, 1801, a quick palace coup put an end to the life—and reign—of Paul I. Consequently, many of the tsar's ambitious plans for the palace at Gatchina were never realized. The palace and town were only awakened again in the second quarter of the nineteenth century, when the military staff of Paul's son, Tsar Nicholas I, was housed there for the first time during the annual maneuvers of the Russian Army. In 1844, the last series of construction works at Gatchina was initiated: two rectangular "blocks" were connected to each side of the main palace. The project, which lasted for six years, was personally overseen by Nicholas I, a first-class engineer in his own right, who suggested new materials such as hollow brick, ceramic ceilings, and terracotta, all of which gave the new sections of the palace a lighter, more up-to-date ambiance.

By mid-century, the palace would not change its appearance again. Tsars Alexander II and Alexander III stayed infrequently and only refurbished their own apartments, barely touching the rooms of their predecessors. Russia's last monarch, Nicholas II, spent even less time at Gatchina. In May of 1917, after the overthrow of the

Romanovs, the Provisional Government decided to make the former imperial residence a museum. After the October Revolution of that year, the government headed by Lenin proclaimed that they would preserve for posterity all of the former royal properties. Nevertheless, by 1920 the Bolsheviks had begun a mass sale of most of the palaces' collections. Out of the 200,000 art objects originally housed at Gatchina, by 1940 only a little over half remained, most having been sold abroad to museums or wealthy Americans such as heiress Marjorie Meriweather Post.

When the Second World War began, the museum staff started evacuating what was left of the collection. Miraculously, they managed to rescue nearly everything: armaments, paintings, precious metals, tapestries, miniatures, bronzeware, and furniture.

The rebirth of the museum began after the liberation of the town of Gatchina on January 26, 1944. The palace had been nearly destroyed by the Nazis, and restoration works were started immediately. It took over forty years of painstaking labor and millions of "dollars" before the central block of the Gatchina Palace was finally ready to receive visitors in 1985. It was only in that year that many of the original furnishings and objects that had been removed for safekeeping to other parts of Russia began to be returned to the palace.

At present, the monumental restoration works are still going on at Gatchina, and the collection is still being returned step by step. The vast park surrounding the palace, the plan of which had not been significantly altered since the end of the eighteenth century, is emerging once again as one of the most beautiful natural settings in all Russia.

Every year, the palace and parks of Gatchina attract more and more visitors. The tours, lectures, and celebrated concerts of classical music continue to make this site one of the most fascinating—and romantic—in the world.

— *Dr. Nikolai S. Tretyakov,*
Director, Gatchina

Having received Gatchina Palace in 1783 as a gift from his mother, Catherine the Great, Grand Duke Paul Petrovich, heir to the throne, could not afford large construction works at his new estate. Besides, he already owned the Grand Duke's Palace at Pavlovsk. Only after November 6, 1796, when Catherine II finally died and Paul inherited the throne, could he begin the large building projects at Gatchina that he had long waited to carry out.

Wasting no time, in the spring of 1797 the new tsar ordered the construction of four throne rooms at Gatchina. Two of them were intended for himself, one for the tsarina, Maria Fyodorovna, and one for his heir, the tsarevich Alexander. The reason for so many throne rooms had more to do with symbolism than need. Having always detested the way his mother had usurped the throne, Paul was obsessed with making sure such a thing would never happen again. One of his first decrees as the new absolute ruler of Russia was an iron-clad "Law of Succession," which from that point forward would guarantee that a tsar's oldest son would always inherit the throne. If there was no male heir, the throne would pass to the ruler's brother. In any case, this new edict made it quite clear that henceforward no woman would sit on the Romanov throne again. The four throne rooms were thus merely a way of publicizing this new law. They demonstrated to all who were received by the tsar at Gatchina that each member of the royal family—tsar, tsarina, and tsarevich—knew his rightful place and took his "absolute" power seriously.

Ironically, the most beautiful of the new rooms, the "Formal" Throne Room of the tsar himself, was situated in the former private library of Count Orlov, the man who had helped murder Paul's father. The new monarch considered it his moral obligation to annihilate any signs of life of the detested count there, especially the times which Catherine II had spent with him. To accomplish these ends, Paul hired the talented Italian architect Vincenzo Brenna to design the Throne Room in a way that might glorify the might and power of the Russian emperor in a solemn and refined manner. There were to be no plafond (ceiling) paintings and little gilt. Instead, the room was painted in the tsar's favorite hues, a flesh-toned pink (or "thigh of a scared nymph," as the shade was poetically called at the time) and lettuce green. Historical references would lend the room a more dignified air. The depiction of a single-headed eagle was obligatory. The walls were embellished with priceless Gobelins tapestries, including "Asia" and "Africa," which had been given to Paul by Louis XVI of France during his trip as grand duke throughout western Europe. Another tapestry, "Ceres," was placed above the room's fireplace, opposite windows which looked out onto the garden. Decorated with magnificent flower garlands on a pink ground, it belonged to a series entitled "Gods."

The central section of the room, of course, was dominated by the throne platform, on which the throne chair has been standing until the present day. Carved of wood, gilded, and upholstered with crimson velvet, this literal "seat" of the Russian government featured the Romanov coat of arms—the double-headed eagle—as well as intricate gold embroidery boasting an unusual Maltese Cross. Although he was the "defender" of the Russian Orthodox Church and the Maltese Order was decidedly Roman Catholic, Paul had long dreamt of a convergence of these two great Christian sects. The Maltese Cross is a fitting testament to this great romantic notion.

Unfortunately, the Throne Room was not quite large enough for many of the official ceremonies held there. To make room for everyone, few pieces of furniture were commissioned for it, the only exceptions being a round bronze table with a blue-gray Urals jasper top and large, white gilt-wood torchères. The room's stunning parquet floor, however, made furniture almost superfluous. Executed in a number of precious woods such as apple, rosewood, mahogany, ebony, and pear, it features a series of interwoven "wreaths" surrounded by an intricate rhombic grid.

The Throne Room of Paul I, one of the most refined and beautiful of any of the eighteenth-century rooms in Russia, remains a testament to the elegant tastes of its proprietor. It is also a testament to that tsar's dearly held belief in his absolute right to rule. Today, thanks to dedicated contemporary artisans, craftsmen, and restorers, we can visit Gatchina and more easily imagine life as it was lived in royal circles almost two hundred years ago.

— *Dr. Nikolai S. Tretyakov*

Palaces of St. Petersburg

JOHANN BAPTISTE
LAMPI THE ELDER.
PORTRAIT OF THE
GRAND DUCHESS
ELENA PAVLOVNA.
1792.
OIL ON CANVAS. 70 X 53.
INV. NO. 154-III.

LEFT:
PORTRAIT OF THE
GRAND DUCHESS
ALEXANDRA
PAVLOVNA. UNKNOWN
PAINTER. LATE 1780S.
OIL ON CANVAS. 50 X 40.
INV. NO. 124-III.
This likeness of the eldest
daughter of Tsar Paul I is
unusual for its juxtaposi-
tion of an elaborate
crown with a simple peas-
ant dress in the Russian
style. The portrait above
is of Alexandra's younger
sister.

RIGHT:
GEORGE DAWE.
PORTRAIT OF THE
GRAND DUKE
ALEXANDER
NIKOLAEVICH AND
THE GRAND DUCHESS
MARIA NIKOLAEVNA.
1821.
OIL ON CANVAS. 135 X
105. INV. NO. 104-III.
This charming painting
of the future Tsar
Alexander II and his
younger sister was kept in
the private apartments of
Nicholas I at Gatchina
until 1941.

Palaces of St. Petersburg

SEMYON FYODOROVICH SHEDRIN. VIEW OF GATCHINA PALACE AND PARK. 1799-1800.

OIL ON CANVAS. 303 X 263. INV. NO. 74-III. One of a series of paintings by the official court landscape artist depicting views of the various imperial parks near St. Petersburg, this canvas captures the arcadian charm of Gatchina's surroundings.

TOP:
SERVICE WITH VIEWS OF GATCHINA PALACE AND PARK. IMPERIAL PORCELAIN WORKS. ST. PETERSBURG. 1850-1875.
PORCELAIN; OVERGLAZE POLYCHROME PAINTING, GOLD PAINTING.

Featuring bucolic views of the assorted palaces, pavilions, and landmarks at Gatchina, the complete ten-piece service includes a decorative "board" depicting the main approach to Gatchina Palace from the "Triple Linden Avenue."

BOTTOM:
"TETE-A-TETE" COFFEE SERVICE OF EMPRESS ALEXANDRA FYODOROVNA. IMPERIAL PORCELAIN WORKS. ST. PETERSBURG. 1820S.
PORCELAIN; GOLD PAINTING, TOOLING, MOLDING.

The complete service of thirty pieces is unusual for its mixed provenance. The original ensemble of superb Meissen, including an ice-cream bowl and tureen (detail opposite), was expanded through the years with examples in the same style from the Imperial Porcelain Works in St. Petersburg.

Palaces of St. Petersburg

**HUNTING GUN.
RUSSIA. MID-1700s.**
STEEL, WOOD, GILDING,
CARVING, ENGRAVING.
LENGTH-79. CALIBRE-
1.3. INV. 760-IX.
With parts crafted in
both Moscow and at the
Imperial Armory Works
in Tula, this elegant rifle
boasts the imperial coat-
of-arms of Empress
Elizabeth Petrovna.

**BELOW, TOP:
HUNTING GUN OF
TSAR ALEXANDER III.
MASTER N. GONNO.
ST. PETERSBURG.
1800S.**
STEEL, WOOD; ENGRAV-
ING. LENGTH-110.
CALIBRE-1. INV. NO.
1041-IX.

**BELOW, BOTTOM:
COSSACK-STYLE
CHILD'S SWORD OF
THE GRAND DUKE
NICHOLAS
ALEXANDROVICH.
MASTER R. ALEXEEV.
ST. PETERSBURG.
1881.**
STEEL, SILVER, GOLD,
LEATHER, WOOD; CARV-
ING, BURNISHING.
LENGTH-76. LENGTH OF
THE BLADE-66. INV. 263-
264-IX.

GOWN OF THE GRAND DUCHESS CATHERINE PAVLOVNA. FRANCE. LATE 1700S.

SILVER SILK BROCADE, VELVET, EMBROIDERY WITH SPANGLES. INV. NOS. 117-119-II.

Featuring the tiny waist, exaggerated hoops, and formal train that were de rigueur for palace balls, this elegant gown worn by the daughter of Tsar Paul I was the height of French fashion at the end of the eighteenth century.

CORONATION THRONE ARMCHAIR OF TSAR ALEXANDER III. RUSSIA. LATE 1800S.

WOOD, GILDING, VELVET, SILK, BROCADE, EMBROIDERY WITH SILVER. 205 X 85 X 75. INV. 53-V.

Upholstery embellished with the double-headed Romanov eagle and the monogram of Alexander III lend an appropriate majesty to this gilded throne chair. Used for the tsar's coronation in 1883, it was displayed at the Moscow Kremlin until 1970.

The magnificent Throne
Room of Paul I, designed
by Vincenzo Brenna in
what was formerly the
private library of Count
Orlov at Gatchina, fea-
tures an ornate throne—
which was refurbished for
this exhibition—and
priceless Gobelins tapes-
tries lining the walls. The
late-nineteenth-century
watercolor above shows
the throne chair's original
embroidery, as well as the
original baldachin and
flanking torchères.

THIS PAGE AND OVERLEAF: TAPESTRIES "ASIA" (TOP AND OVERLEAF) AND "AFRICA" (BOTTOM). ROYAL TAPESTRY MANUFACTORY (GOBELINS). PARIS. 1750-1780.
WOOL, SILK. 499 X 373. INV. NOS. 169-170-II. These remarkable Gobelins tapestries, woven in Paris after paintings by the early French landscape artist Alexandre-François Desportes, depict the exotic flora and fauna of two continents and feature the use of the exquisite "Gobelins Blue" dye.

LEFT:
THRONE ARMCHAIR AND STOOL OF TSAR PAUL I. MASTER H. MEYER. ST. PETERSBURG. 1797.
WOOD, GILDING, VELVET, EMBROIDERY. 180 X 90 X 70. INV. NO. I-V. One of six crafted for Paul I, this throne chair was transferred in 1970 from the Armory of the Kremlin in Moscow to the Throne Room at Gatchina to replace the original that had been lost during WWII. That original's embroidery, which had featured the double-headed imperial eagle and an unusual Maltese Cross, was re-created specially for the present exhibition.

Palaces of St. Petersburg

**TRIPOD TABLE.
RUSSIA. 1700s.**

GILDED BRONZE, GRAY-
BLUE URALS JASPER,
COBALT-BLUE GLASS.
HEIGHT-84. DIAMETER-
106. INV. NO. 36-VIII.
In order to accommodate
large audiences with the
tsar, the Throne Room of
Paul I was always kept
sparely furnished. One
exception was this
extremely elegant gilded-
bronze table with a top of
rare Urals jasper and an
ornamental vase of
cobalt-blue glass under-
neath. It was used to hold
official documents await-
ing the tsar's imperial seal
and signature.

Palaces of St. Petersburg

Pavlovsk

The palace and park ensemble of Pavlovsk was the last of the chief imperial residences to be created in the environs of St. Petersburg. Although the whole complex was constructed in a rather short span of time—a little more than fifty years—it is nevertheless distinguished by a particularly harmonious unity of architecture, sculpture, and landscape design.

Picturesquely situated on the banks of the Slavyanka River south of the capital, Pavlovsk, like the palace of Versailles in France, was originally a modest hunting lodge where the Russian monarchs could engage in one of their favorite pastimes. All of that changed in 1777, when Catherine the Great presented the property to her son and heir, Paul (Pavel) Petrovich, to commemorate the birth of her first grandson, the tsarevich Alexander. A great lover of the arts—one of the few qualities he inherited from his mother—Paul immediately set out to transform the modest estate into a residence befitting his status as a grand duke. He hired the best architects and artists who were then working in Russia, including Charles Cameron, Pietro Gonzaga, Vincenzo Brenna, Paolo Visconti, Giacomo Quarenghi, Thomas de Thomon, and Carlo Rossi. With a spirit of freedom they were unable to exercise in their native countries, these imaginative foreigners were able, one after another, to fully realize their creative potential in Russia. At the same time, the master Russian craftsmen and artisans who helped them were able to absorb a vast knowledge of western European culture and design. The result was a palace uniquely Russian in its melding of western and native vernaculars.

The neo-classical boudoir of Empress Maria Fyodorovna at Pavlovsk includes a splendid suite of furniture designed by the Russian master Andrei Voronikhin, including this Egyptian-themed armchair (1805) featured in the present exhibition.

The first stage of Pavlovsk's construction (1782-1796) was largely the work of Cameron, the brilliant Scottish architect and connoisseur of antiquity. His remarkable designs for what was originally planned as a country residence for Grand Duke Paul and his family combined elements of Italian Palladian architecture with those of native Russian country-house design. The main block, three-storied and decorated with columned porticos, was linked to side wings by semicircles of open galleries. In the center and visible from a great distance, a Palladian-style dome crowned the whole structure.

Inside, all of the rooms were decorated in neo-classical simplicity by Cameron. Only

five of the ground-floor rooms are Cameron's work today, however, because the Italian Vincenzo Brenna was soon brought in to refurbish the palace's interiors in a more grandiose style to suit Grand Duchess Maria Fyodorovna's tastes. In place of the sophisticated simplicity of Cameron's sensibility, Brenna's style was more full-blown. His interiors were filled with decorative elements, furniture, and objects of neo-Egyptian and Roman design, as well as with the military-themed paraphernalia of which Paul was so fond.

After the death of Catherine II in 1796 and Paul's ascent to the throne, the idyllic estate was expanded again. Another story was added to the side wings, and a palace chapel was constructed. It was the names of Quarenghi, Voronikhin, and Rossi, however, which soon marked the longest phase of the palace's ongoing expansion. In 1800, Quarenghi redecorated the private rooms on the ground floor, including the New Study of Paul I, the Pilaster Study, and the Boudoir of Maria Fyodorovna. In January of 1803, a terrible fire completely destroyed the interiors of the "State" rooms of the central block, and Andrei Voronikhin, a Russian who had apprenticed with the best western European masters, was invited for their restoration. Among his works was the redesign of the Lantern Study in Maria Fyodorovna's wing, which has been re-created for the present exhibition (and which is discussed more fully in the following section). Still later—in the 1820s—Rossi was invited to Pavlovsk to create the magnificent library over the northern gallery of the palace. By 1824, the appearance of Pavlovsk Palace would change no more. And although Cameron, Brenna, Quarenghi, Voronikhin, and Rossi all worked on different phases of the palace's construction—each adding his own signature to the design—the structure as a whole is still considered the most perfect—and unified—example of Russian classicism.

As far as the furnishing of Pavlovsk was concerned, that task fell largely to the palace's proprietors themselves, both of whom shared a cultivation largely acquired on a "grand tour" of Italy and France undertaken soon after their marriage. On that seminal trip, Paul Petrovich and Maria Fyodorovna had used every opportunity to meet with the artists, sculptors, bronzesmiths, and furniture masters whom they thought they might like to commission for work at Pavlovsk. They also collected hundreds of decorative objects with which to furnish their favorite residence.

Lovely paintings by Jean-Baptiste Greuze, Claude Joseph Vernet, and Angelica Kauffmann, as well as stunning architectural landscapes by Hubert Robert, soon decorated the palace. In a Picture Gallery specially designed by Brenna, canvases by Italian, French, Flemish, and Dutch masters were hung chock-a-block on the walls. The collection of sculpture was also first-rate, including works by Italian masters and replicas brilliantly executed by Russian artisans. Tapestries created at the celebrated Royal

Tapestry Works (Gobelins) in Paris adorned the palace's empty walls, and priceless Savonnerie carpets covered exquisitely crafted floors.

One of the prize collections of the palace was the exquisite porcelain gathered by the tsarina from every corner of the globe. A particularly important sixty-piece toilet set originally commissioned by Marie Antoinette and inscribed with the French queen's coat of arms was displayed in the State Bedroom, and pieces by such celebrated porcelain houses as Meissen, Wedgwood, Ludwigsburg, and Sèvres (not to mention the Imperial Porcelain Works in St. Petersburg!) filled tabletops and vitrines throughout the imperial compound.

The palace also housed—and still does—the best collection of illumination devices of any of the royal residences. Chandeliers, lamps, sconces, candelabra, and girandoles were commissioned for every room of Pavlovsk, and Andrei Voronikhin himself designed a new kind of lamp suspended from delicately wrought chains which replaced many of the lighting fixtures lost in the fire of 1803.

Of all the imperial residences, Pavlovsk is also rightfully celebrated for the consistently high quality of its furniture. The tsar and tsarina commissioned peerless masters such as Henri Jacob in Paris and David Roentgen in Berlin to execute original designs, including the former's imposing gilt-wood and silk-upholstered garniture for the State Bedroom.

Rounding out these luxurious ensembles of paintings, porcelain, and furniture was a magnificent assortment of objets d'art, including a unique collection of jewel-like steel objects from Tula (Russia), a peerless collection of Russian and European artistic bronzeware by masters such as Pierre-Philippe Thomire, and a fabulous number of mantel and table clocks, so meticulously crafted that most of them still keep time to this day.

OVERLEAF:
The Italian architect Vincenzo Brenna created the imposing Picture Gallery at Pavlovsk in the late eighteenth century in order to house the important collection of paintings by Italian, French, Flemish, and Dutch masters that Tsar Paul I and his wife had amassed during their travels throughout Europe. The room also features a number of finely wrought neo-classical decorative objects, such as the unusual porphyry and gilded-bronze vase with goat-head handles in the foreground of the photograph.

All of these remarkable collections were formed mainly during the lifetime of Maria Fyodorovna. The subsequent proprietors of the palace, although they did not make any essential contributions to the collections, at least managed to carefully preserve them. After the revolution of 1917, Pavlovsk, along with the other royal palaces in or near St. Petersburg, was transformed into a museum. The following quarter of a century was marked by a series of seemingly insurmountable obstacles, none of which, however, approached the severity of the palace's occupation by the Germans in WWII. Pavlovsk was almost entirely destroyed by fire, and the park was laid waste by trenches and mines. Luckily, at the end of the conflict, Pavlovsk was one of the first palaces to

receive funds for restoration works. After a grueling amount of labor, the park was able to receive visitors again by 1950. Today, the restoration of the palace is still continuing. At present, forty-five of the principal rooms have been completed, and the future of Pavlovsk is finally beginning to look as bright as its splendid past.

— *Dr. Yuri V. Mudrov,*
Director, Pavlovsk

LANTERN STUDY

After Paul I was tragically killed in a palace coup in 1801, his widow, the Empress Maria Fyodorovna, began spending almost the entire year at Pavlovsk. In order to obliterate the tragic memories certain rooms held of her husband, she decided to decorate anew many of her private apartments. She invited two architects to fulfill the task: Giacomo Quarenghi, who had already worked at Pavlovsk, and Andrei Voronikhin, who had been introduced to the tsarina by her friend Count Alexander Stroganov.

In the end, it was Voronikhin who became the chief designer of Maria Fyodorovna's new suite of rooms. This talented Russian designed not only the interiors, but also much of the rooms' furniture, lamps, decorative vases, and assorted odds and ends. A serf who was born on the estate of the enlightened Count Stroganov, Voronikhin acquired a brilliant education, including a training course at the studio of the famous Moscow architect Matvei Kazakov. In 1789, Stroganov's ambitious ward even made a trip with the count to France, where they both visited the celebrated workshop of Percier and Fontaine, two of Napoleon's favorite architects.

Eventually liberated from his serfdom, Voronikhin became the personal architect of Stroganov's family and later began giving lectures at the Academy of Fine Arts in St. Petersburg, where he soon won the coveted title of "Academician."

In 1803, after a great fire ravaged Pavlovsk, Count Stroganov recommended Voronikhin to the still-grieving widow of Paul I. It was at Pavlovsk that the rich talents of Voronikhin were finally able to flower into a style completely his own. And in none of the rooms he refurbished for Maria Fyodorovna was that style better illustrated than in the Lantern Study, the gem of the singularly Russian brand of neo-classicism that Voronikhin was largely responsible for creating.

Boasting a large bow window and a coffered semi-dome ceiling supported by four Ionic columns faced with white stucco, this elegant space is pierced by large windows looking out on the tsarina's private garden, the whole creating a sense of unity with nature. A study in contrast between light and dark, the sunlight-flooded room features white walls and bookshelves that serve as dramatic counterpoints to the black and gold colors of the painted furniture.

As in the other rooms at Pavlovsk, paintings form an important element of the decor, with canvases by European masters of the sixteenth to seventeenth centuries such as Francesco Albani, Carlo Dolci, and Guido Reni (Italian School) and Charles Le Brun, Pierre Mignard, and Sebastien Bourdon (French School) lining the walls. The masterpiece of the collection is Agnolo Bronzino's sixteenth-century *Madonna and Child With John the Baptist*.

In the middle of the study stands a mahogany bureau by David Roentgen, one of the most celebrated European cabinetmakers of the eighteenth century. On it are displayed exquisite nineteenth-century accessories, such as a crystal inkset, "miracle" candlestick, and a bronze and malachite paperweight. Furnishings after Voronikhin's own designs fill out the decor, with a gorgeously patterned inlaid floor unifying the whole ensemble.

During the Second World War, the Lantern Study was completely destroyed. Painstakingly re-created in the 1960s with the use of archive documents and historical photographs, today it is a vivid testament to Voronikhin's genius and one of the most charming rooms of any palace in Russia.

—Ludmila V. Koval,
Deputy Director, Pavlovsk

RIGHT:
The architectural highlight of Andrei Voronikhin's classically inspired Lantern Study at Pavlovsk, re-created for the present exhibition, is the luminous bow window with a coffered half-dome ceiling supported by four Ionic columns and graceful caryatids in antique robes.

WASTEPAPER BASKET. DESIGN BY ANDREI VORONIKHIN. WORKSHOP OF HEINRICH GAMBS. ST. PETERSBURG. 1812. MAHOGANY VENEERING, CARVING, GILDING, SILK-ON-CANVAS EMBROIDERY IN CROSS-STITCH. 71 X 74 X 40. INV. NO. ZX-653-V. So tailored were the rooms Voronikhin designed at Pavlovsk that even objects as mundane as a wastepaper basket were fashioned by the very best artisans. This elegant example originally graced the Rose Pavilion and now sits beside Empress Maria Fyodorovna's writing desk in the Lantern Study.

Palaces of St. Petersburg

This ensemble of furniture gracing one wall of the Lantern Study at Pavlovsk includes an important late-eighteenth-century mahogany desk from the celebrated workshop of David Roentgen. On it are displayed some of the accessories considered de rigueur for a lady's study of the day: a Russian-designed "miracle" candlestick with watercolor scene, a green Morocco casket-blotting pad, as well as a double-column amber-and-ivory table decoration designed by Grand Duchess Maria Fyodorovna and inscribed with her and her husband's monograms. Above the desk hang a number of religious-themed seventeenth-century French- and Italian-school oil paintings.

WRITING SET. IMPERIAL GLASS WORKS. ST. PETERSBURG. 1810S.
CRYSTAL, "DIAMOND" CUT. BASE: HEIGHT-6. LENGTH-26. WIDTH-20.2. INK-POT, SAND-BOX, AND FEATHER-VASE: HEIGHT-8.8.
Adorning Empress Maria Fyodorovna's desk in the Lantern Study, this four-piece writing set, like all of the objects on this and the following page, was commissioned expressly by architect Andrei Voronikhin for that room.

TRIPOD JARDINIERE (ONE OF A PAIR). ST. PETERSBURG. 1800-1825.
MAHOGANY, BLUE GLASS, METAL. HEIGHT-93. DIAMETER-29. INV. NO. 1109-V.

PAPERWEIGHT. PETERHOF LAPIDARY WORKS. EARLY 1800S.
GILDED BRONZE, MALACHITE; "RUSSIAN MOSAIC," GRINDING, POLISHING, CHASING. HEIGHT-15. BASE-4.2 X 15 X 9. INV. NO. 3931-IV.

Palaces of St. Petersburg

VASE WITH BRONZE HANDLES IN THE FORM OF SATYRS' MASKS (ONE OF A PAIR). DESIGN BY GIACOMO QUARENGHI. PETERHOF LAPIDARY WORKS. 1800.
JASPER, GILDED BRONZE; GRINDING, POLISHING, CASTING, CHASING, GILDING. HEIGHT-46. DIAMETER-22. INV. NO. 594-VIII.

ARMCHAIR (ONE OF A PAIR). DESIGN BY ANDREI VORONIKHIN. ST. PETERSBURG. 1807.
PAINTED AND GILDED WOOD, EMBROIDERY. 101 X 64 X 61. INV. NO. 372-V.
This graceful Empire-style armchair was originally upholstered in a luxurious light-blue silk ornamented with embroidered bees. That original fabric has since been lost.

BOWL WITH SITTING SATYR. AFTER THE drawing BY S. S. PIMENOV. BRONZE WORKSHOP AT THE ACADEMY OF FINE ARTS. PETERHOF LAPIDARY WORKS. 1809.
MARBLE, GILDED AND PATINATED BRONZE; GRINDING, POLISHING, CASTING, CHASING, GILDING. HEIGHT-29.3. DIAMETER-23. INV. NO. 666-VIII.

VASE WITH VIEWS OF VENICE (ONE OF A PAIR). UNMARKED. IMPERIAL PORCELAIN WORKS. ST. PETERSBURG. 1790S. PORCELAIN, OVERGLAZE COVERING WITH CERISE LUSTRE, OVERGLAZE POLYCHROME PAINTING, GOLD RELIEF, TOOLING. HEIGHT-37. DIAMETER-27. INV. NO. ZX-7097-I.

BUST OF TSAR ALEXANDER I. CHRISTIAN DANIEL RAUCH. GERMANY. 1818. WHITE MARBLE. HEIGHT-61.5. LENGTH-41. WIDTH-26.5. INV. NO. ZX-251-VIII.

RIGHT: AGNOLO BRONZINO. MADONNA AND CHILD WITH JOHN THE BAPTIST. ITALY. 1500S OIL ON PANEL. 100 X 79. The most important of Pavlovsk's extensive collection of sixteenth- and seventeenth-century French and Italian paintings, this Renaissance masterpiece was originally commissioned by the grand duke of Tuscany, Cosimo I de' Medici, for his palace in Florence. It now hangs in the Lantern Study.

GUIDO RENI. ARCHANGEL GABRIEL OF THE ANNUNCIATION. ITALY. 1600s.
OIL ON CANVAS. 58 X 47. INV. NO. ZX-1827-III. Strongly influenced by the works of Caravaggio, Reni, the head of the prestigious Accademia dell' Arte in Bologna, executed this canvas as a companion to the *Virgin of the Annunciation*, above. Both paintings were presented by Tsar Nicholas I to his mother, the Dowager Empress Maria Fyodorovna, who hung them in the Lantern Study.

GUIDO RENI. VIRGIN OF THE ANNUNCIATION. ITALY. 1600s.
OIL ON CANVAS. 58.5 X 47. INV. NO. ZX-1828-III.

CARLO DOLCI. <u>SAINT SEBASTIAN</u>. ITALY. **1600s.**
OIL ON CANVAS. 80 X 64.5. INV. NO. ZX-1906-III.

CARLO DOLCI. <u>MARY MAGDALENE</u>. ITALY. **1600s.**
OIL ON CANVAS. 87.5 X 73.8. INV. NO. ZX-1901-III.

Florentine master Carlo Dolci's melodramatic interpretation of the Christian saints made his work extremely popular with Russian collectors, especially Empress Maria Fyodorovna, who purchased the two canvases on this page for the Lantern Study at Pavlovsk.

FRANCESCO ALBANI.
THE HOLY FAMILY
RESTING DURING THE
FLIGHT INTO EGYPT.
ITALY. 1600s.
OIL ON CANVAS. 65 X 73.
INV. NO. ZX-1920-III.
Purchased by the Grand
Duke Michael Pavlovich
in 1819 in Naples as a gift
for his mother, the
Dowager Empress Maria
Fyodorovna, this late-
Renaissance Italian canvas
hangs above the
Empress's writing desk in
the Lantern Study.

RIGHT:
ABRAHAM VAN
DIEPENBECK. THE
CHURCH FATHERS.
SCHOOL OF RUBENS.
FLANDERS. 1600s.
OIL ON CANVAS. 64 X 47.
INV. NO. ZX-1916-III.

Palaces of St. Petersburg

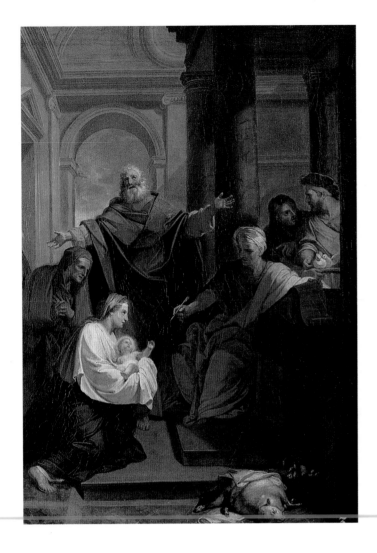

JEAN JOUVENET. **THE PRESENTATION IN THE TEMPLE**. FRANCE. **1600s.**
OIL ON CANVAS. 73.5 X 54.2. INV. NO. ZX-1927-III.
This mannered canvas by Jouvenet, a student of Charles Le Brun and a favorite at the French court of Louis XIV, was purchased in 1772 by Catherine the Great for the Winter Palace in St. Petersburg.

BENEDETTO LUTI. **MADONNA AND CHILD**. ITALY. **1600s.**
OIL ON CANVAS. 85 X 67. INV. NO. ZX-1589-III.

PIERRE MIGNARD.
CHRIST AND THE
SAMARITAN WOMAN.
FRANCE. 1600S.
OIL ON CANVAS. 38 X 49.
INV. NO. ZX-1903-III.
The director of the
Academie Royale and the
Gobelins tapestry works
in Paris, Mignard was
commissioned by Louis
XIV to execute this reli-
gious-themed canvas,
which was later pur-
chased by Catherine the
Great for her personal
collection.

CHARLES LE BRUN.
MATER DOLOROSA.
FRANCE. 1600S.
OIL ON CANVAS. 56 X 46.
INV. NO. ZX-1905-III.

SEBASTIEN BOURDON.
LUCIUS ALBINUS
OFFERING HIS
CHARIOT TO THE
VESTAL VIRGINS
DURING THE FIRE OF
ROME. FRANCE.
1600s.

OIL ON CANVAS. 24 X 32.
INV. NO. ZX-1924-III.
The classical theme of
this small canvas by
Bourdon, at one time the
official court portrait
painter for Queen
Christina of Sweden,
appealed to the neo-clas-
sical tastes of Empress
Maria Fyodorovna, who
purchased it for the
Lantern Study in 1807.

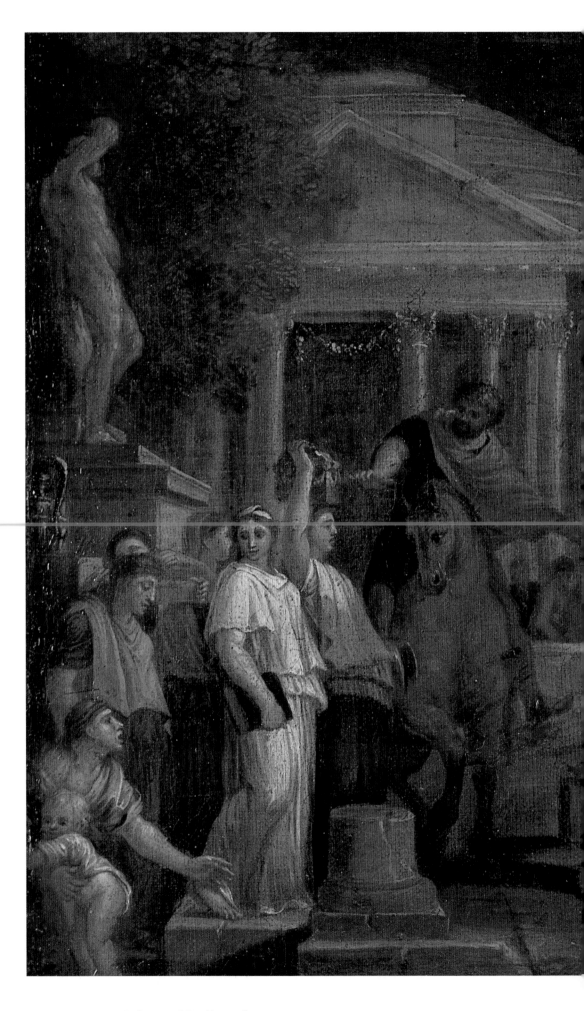

Palaces of St. Petersburg

Palaces of St. Petersburg

HUBERT ROBERT.
ANTIQUE RUINS OF
ROME. FRANCE.
1786.
OIL ON CANVAS. 208 X
291. INV. NO. ZX-1622-
III.
A distinguished French
landscape architect and a
painter celebrated for his
idealized landscapes and
fantastic ruins, Robert
was commissioned by
Grand Duke Paul
Petrovich to execute
three large compositions,
including this one, for
the halls of the
Kamennoostrovsky Palace
in St. Petersburg. The
entire series now hangs at
Pavlovsk.

OPPOSITE:
ALEXANDER ROSLIN.
PORTRAIT OF THE
GRAND DUCHESS
MARIA FYODOROVNA.
1777.
OIL ON CANVAS. 245 X
167. INV. NO. ZX-3749-
III.
A replica by Roslin of a
canvas he had originally
painted for the Winter
Palace by order of
Catherine the Great, this
appropriately elegant por-
trait of the future tsarina
is a fitting tribute to
Pavlovsk's most cultivated
proprietress.

Palaces of St. Petersburg

BUREAU-JARDINIERE. DESIGN BY ANDREI VORONIKHIN. WORKSHOP OF HEINRICH GAMBS. ST. PETERSBURG. 1803. MAHOGANY VENEERING, GILDED AND PATINATED BRONZE, BRASS, ZINC, GLASS, EMBROIDERY. 120 X 123 X 56. INV. NO. 376-V.

ABOVE AND RIGHT: ARMCHAIR. DESIGN BY ANDREI VORONIKHIN. ST. PETERSBURG. 1805. PAINTED AND GILDED WOOD; TAPESTRY UPHOLSTERY. 96 X 73 X 64. INV. NO. 311-V. The first to introduce Egyptian motifs to Russian design, Voronikhin designed much of the furniture for Empress Maria Fyodorovna's boudoir at Pavlovsk, including this elaborate sphinx-legged armchair featuring the original tapestry upholstery woven in Beauvais, France.

DRESSING TABLE OF CATHERINE THE GREAT. TULA, RUSSIA. 1787. STEEL, GILDED BRONZE, GOLD; INLAID PATTERN, BURNISHING, POLISHING, CHASING. TABLE: 116 X 72 X 67. MIRROR: HEIGHT-71. BASE-48 X 24. POWDER VASES: HEIGHT-37. DIAMETER-20. OBELISKS: HEIGHT-53. INV. NOS. 746-752-VIII.

SETTEE, CHAIR, AND ARMCHAIR. DESIGN BY ANDREI VORONIKHIN. ST. PETERSBURG. C. 1805.
MAHOGANY, CARVING, GILDING, PAINTING IN IMITATION BRONZE, EMBROIDERY.
SETTEE: 94 X 179 X 54.
CHAIR: 92 X 48 X 49.

ARMCHAIR: 92 X 53 X 51.
INV. NOS. 1083, 1085, 1089-V.
Designed by Voronikhin for the Pilaster Study at Pavlovsk, this unusual suite of furniture with gilded serpent-motif backs boasts the original embroidered seat cushions.

TRIPOD VASE "ATHENIENNE" (ONE OF A PAIR). DESIGN BY ANDREI VORONIKHIN. IMPERIAL GLASS WORKS. ST. PETERSBURG. EARLY 1800s.
CRYSTAL, "DIAMOND" CUT, BLUE GLASS, GILDED BRONZE. HEIGHT-68.
DIAMETER-43. INV. NO. ZX-9864-I.

ABOVE AND RIGHT: TRIPOD TABLE. UNMARKED. IMPERIAL PORCELAIN WORKS. ST. PETERSBURG. 1798.
PORCELAIN; UNDERGLAZE COBALT PAINTING, OVER-GLAZE POLYCHROME PAINTING, GILDED AND PATINATED BRONZE. HEIGHT-74. DIAMETER-50. INV. NO. ZX-4078-IV.
This neo-classical table with lion-paw legs includes an intricately designed top featuring a landscape scene at Pavlovsk after Semyon Shedrin's watercolor *The Ruin and the Black Bridge* surrounded by a triple border of interwoven branches, golden ornament, and mixed flowers.

VASE WITH GOAT-HEAD HANDLES (ONE OF A PAIR). BRONZE WORKSHOP OF THE ACADEMY OF FINE ARTS. KOLYVAN LAPIDARY WORKS. RUSSIA. 1789. PORPHYRY, GILDED BRONZE; GRINDING, POLISHING, CASTING, CHASING, GILDING. 79 X 51 X 38. INV. NO. 953-VIII.

BOWL WITH BRONZE
FALCONS AND
RIBBONS. DESIGN BY
ANDREI VORONIKHIN.
BRONZE WORKSHOP
OF THE ACADEMY OF
FINE ARTS.
EKATERINBURG
LAPIDARY WORKS.
RUSSIA. 1807.
JASPER, GILDED BRONZE;
GRINDING, POLISHING,
CASTING, CHASING.
HEIGHT-47.5. DIAMETER-
34.5. INV. NO. 612-VIII.

Palaces of St. Petersburg

STONE VASE WITH
SNAKE-SHAPED
HANDLES (ONE OF A
PAIR). DESIGN BY
ANDREI VORONIKHIN.
BRONZE WORKSHOP
OF THE ACADEMY OF
FINE ARTS.
EKATERINBURG
LAPIDARY WORKS.
RUSSIA. 1801-1802.
JASPER, GILDED BRONZE;
GRINDING, POLISHING,
CHASING, GILDING.
HEIGHT-67. DIAMETER
WITH HANDLES-40.5. INV.
NO. 958-VIII.

Palaces of St. Petersburg

**BOWL WITH
EGYPTIAN FIGURE.
DESIGN BY ANDREI
VORONIKHIN.
BRONZE WORKSHOP
OF THE ACADEMY OF
FINE ARTS. PETERHOF
LAPIDARY WORKS.
RUSSIA. 1809.**
GRANITE, PATINATED
BRONZE; GRINDING, POL-
ISHING, CASTING, CHAS-
ING. HEIGHT-101.
DIAMETER OF THE BOWL-
56. INV. NO. 4102-IV.

Palaces of St. Petersburg

TAPESTRY "THE
TEMPLE OF
FRIENDSHIP AT
PAVLOVSK PARK."
AFTER THE PAINTING
BY SEMYON SHEDRIN.
ST. PETERSBURG
TAPESTRY
MANUFACTORY.
1790S.
WOOL, SILK; 10-11
THREADS PER ONE CM.
150 X 139. INV. NO. ZX-
4842-II.

TABLE DECORATION
WITH COLUMNS. THE
GRAND DUCHESS
MARIA FYODOROVNA
AND N. VAYE. ST.
PETERSBURG. 1792.
IVORY, AMBER, WOOD,
GOLD; TURNERY. 21 X 32
X 20. INV. NO. 294-X.
Designed by the wife of
the future Tsar Paul I,
this ivory and amber
piece includes her and
her husband's mono-
grams ("MF" and "PP")
on the center column. It
now sits atop Maria
Fyodorovna's desk in the
Lantern Study.

RIGHT:
TAPESTRY "THE
APOLLO COLONNADE
AT PAVLOVSK PARK."
AFTER THE PAINTING
BY SEMYON SHEDRIN.
ST. PETERSBURG
TAPESTRY
MANUFACTORY.
1790S.
WOOL, SILK; 10-11
THREADS PER ONE CM.
153 X 139. INV. NO. ZX-
4843-II.

MISSISSIPPI COMMISSION FOR INTERNATIONAL CULTURAL EXCHANGE, INC.

EXECUTIVE COMMITTEE:
Mr. William L. "Buck" Stevens, Chairman•Mr. William D. Mounger, Honorary Chairman
Mr. Thomas B. Shepherd, III•Mr. Douglas C. Rule•Mr. Thomas Pittman•Mr. Daniel G. Hise, General Counsel
Jack L. Kyle, Executive Director

ADVISORY BOARD:
Mr. Rayford R. Hudson•Dr. Aubrey K. Lucas•Mr. Joseph Jackson•Mr. W. H. Holman, Jr.•Mr. Michael Stevens•Ms. Jean Chisholm Lindsey•Mr. Dudley J. Hughes•Mr. Donald E. Meiners•Mr. Matthew L. Holleman•Mr. Frank R. Day•Mr. E. B. Robinson, Jr.•Fred McMillan, M.D.•Mr. Leland R. Speed•Mr. J. Kelly Allgood•Mr. Alton Turnipseed•Dr. Walter Washington•Mr. Aubrey B. Patterson•Mr. N. L. Carson•Ms. Betsy Bradley•The Honorable Marshall Bennett•Mr. Duane McCallister•Ms. Melia Peavey•Mr. Warren A. Hood•Mr. Bill Loveless•Wallace A. Conerly, M.D.•Mr. Ronald Louis Taylor•Ms. Susan Harrison•Robert R. Smith, M.D.•Mrs. Graham Somerville•Mr. George A. Schloegel•Mr. William H. Cooke, Jr.•Mr. William M. Jones•Mr. James L. Moore

EX-OFFICIO
Governor and Mrs. Kirk Fordice•The Honorable Kane Ditto•Mr. Mark Garriga•Mr. James B. Heidel•Mr. George P. Smith•Mr. Vaughn Stinson•Mr. Steve Watson

STAFF:
Jack L. Kyle, Executive Director•William M. Jones, Fund Raising Consultant•Maureen H. Herring, Assistant to the Executive Director•Linda P. Walsh, Director of Finance•Donald T. Sullivan, Director of Security•Kenneth C. Boone, Director of Operations•Candace Crecink, Director of Volunteers•Kimberly Stamps, Assistant Director of Volunteers•Donette D. Lee, Director of Special Projects•Hattie S. Ruder, Director of Sales•Jorge Davis, Sales Office Manager•Leslie Deddens, Group Sales Coordinator•Amy Holaday, School Sales Coordinator•Clinton I. Bagley, School Sales Coordinator•Rifaat Hassan, Gift Shop Manager•Allie Crawford, Ticket Supervisor•Elizabeth Penny, Administrative Assistant•Vera Levitskaja, Assistant to the Executive Director/St. Petersburg•Andre Peshehodko, Assistant/St. Petersburg.

ARCHITECTS & ENGINEERS
Cooke Douglass Farr Lemons, Ltd
William H. Cooke, Jr.•Eric Tscherter•Betsy Bean

EXHIBITION DESIGN & INSTALLATION
Quenroe & Associates
ElRoy E. Quenroe
Charles E. Mack

PACKING, SHIPPING & HANDLING
Haskenkamp International
Hans E. Schneider, President
Diedmar Hardekopf, Project Director
Ilja W. Santowski, Interpreter/Coordinator

GENERAL CONTRACTORS
J. A. Moss Construction Company, Inc.
James A. Moss, President
Advance Manufacturing Co., Inc.

David A. Craig, President
M & M Services, Inc.
Dale McGuffie, President

INTERNATIONAL FREIGHT FORWARDER/
CUSTOM HOUSE BROKER
Alexander International
LeRoy Pettyjohn, Vice President/Export Division

CATERER
MMI Dining Systems, R. J. Cockayne

ADVERTISING
The Ramey Agency, Inc.
Robert M. Austin, II, President & COO

RECORDED TOUR
Antenna Audio
Chris Tellis, Audio Tours Director

Palaces of St. Petersburg

Russian Organizing Committee

PETERHOF:
Vadim V. Znamenov, Director•Nina Vernova, Deputy Director
Scientific Assistants: Elena Gerasimenko•Nelli Melnikova•Marina Trubanovskaya
Restorers: Roman Korolev•Vladimir Tomilin•Galina Fiodorova•Konstantin Khruchov•Polish firm "PKZ"

CATHERINE PALACE AT TSARSKOJE SELO:
Ivan P. Sautov, Director•Victor M. Faybisovitch, Scientific Director•Larisa V. Bardovskaya, Chief Curator
Boris Podolsky, Vice Director on Restoration
Participants: T. F. Boulgakova•G.E. Vyedensky•N.A. Shmeliova•T.M. Boutyrina•N.S. Grirorovich•S.M. Ivanova
L.M. Kanaeva•A. T. Kolesnikova•S.V. Chabutkin•O.F. Filimonova•Z.I. Golubitskaya
Restorers: Firm "Gelikon, Ltd.," V.N. Shapov, Director
Carvers: V.A. Bogdanov•Y.M. Kozlov•A.V. Vinogradov•S.P. Burakov•V.A. Afonichev•S.V. Burnvtsev
Y.I. Fufaev•V.G. Korovanov•V.V. Sazonov
Gilders: T.N. Kozhukhar•I.Y. Basiul•T.A. Lazareva•N.M. Fomichiova•M.N. Miroshinskaya•I.A. Yakunina
Plasterers: Y.A. Cherednilov•V.A. Cherednikov•N.P. Burlova•L.P. Burlova•I.N. Tarasova•L.M. Shyetskaia
Parquet Makers: P.V. Kuliashov•N.V. Konetsky•A.G. Mons•Firm "Continent-2, Ltd.," E. A. Dorfman, Director
G.A. Filatenko•A.F. Lavrov•M.I. Efimkin•A.V. Rylov•I.N. Pikushin•G.V. Golubev

GATCHINA:
Nikolai S. Tretyakov, Director•Tatyana Kozlova, Vice Director•Galina N. Kondakova, Vice Director
Scientific Assistants: G. Kondakova•A. Yolkina•V. Valentina•V. Fyodorova•W. Samceneva•E. Mekeryehova
E. Artemieva•V. Yantsova•G. Tanaevskaya•I. Ryzhendo
Curators of the Restoration Work: E. Krasnov•G. Manzatu•V. Kirpichyov•B. Khitrov•A. Shaureupov
Parquet-makers: S. Komkov•N. Pashenko•V. Shoulepov
Carvers: V. Pesterev•V. Vasiliev•D. Vorotyntsev•I. Patourin•I. Volkov
Carpenter: V. Goloubev
Paintings Restorers: L. Lavroukhina•V. Losev
Restorers of Imperial Gowns: N. Pinyagina•T. Kelyadina
Painter on Fabrics: T. Slizina
Plasterers: A. Zhabin•L. Strizhyova
Painters on Metal: I. Ryseva•S. Petrov

PAVLOVSK:
Yuri V. Mudrov, Director•Ludmila Koval, Scientific Director•Alexei Gusanov, Chief Curator
Restorers: Igor Pikkiev, painting•Leonid Karavaey, Wasiliy Angelov, clocks, bronzeware•Tatiana Telukova,
furniture•Valentina Soldatova, porcelain

Catalogue Staff

Designer:
J.C. Suarès

Project Editor:
J. Spencer Beck

Production:
Alexandra Littlehales

Writers:
Peterhof: Vadim Znamenov (Peterhof, porcelain, glass), Nina Vernova (Yellow Banqueting Hall, paintings, precious metals), Elena Gerasimenko (furniture), Peter Makho (paintings), Tamara Nosovitch (porcelain, glass), Natalia Sergeeva (rare books), Zoya Tikhonravova (applied art, fabrics), Tatiana Khoruzhaya (metal), Vil' Yumangulov (sculpture)

Catherine Palace: Galena D. Khodasevich (Catherine Palace), T. F. Boulgakova (Portrait Hall), T. M. Boutyrina (Blue Formal Drawing Room), L. V. Bardovskaya (painting), G. E. Vvedensky (armaments), N. S. Grigorovich (decorative applied art), L. M. Kanayeva (furniture), A. T. Kolesnikova (fabrics, carriages), V. F. Plaude (photo materials)

Gatchina: Nikolai S. Tretyakov

Pavlovsk: Yuri V. Mudrov (Pavlovsk), Ludmila V. Koval (Lantern Study)